MARIE-FRANCE BOTTE
WITH JEAN-PAUL MARI

The Price of a Child

Four years in the hell of
child prostitution in Bangkok

Original title: *Le Prix d'un Enfant - 4 ans dans l'enfer de la prostitution enfantine à Bangkok, Marie-France Botte avec Jean-Paul Mari.*

Copyright © Editions Robert Laffont, S.A. Paris, 1993

English Translation

by

Edwina Shoucair Maffei

Permission has been granted by the Publisher to Edwina Shoucair Maffei acting on behalf of **Soroptimist International** to publish this translation.

All proceeds from the English language edition of ***The Price of a Child*** for a one-year period will go to the **Soroptimist International** quadrennial project in northern Thailand, involving the education of young girls.

ISBN: 0-9699785-0-2

Front Cover Photograph: Micheline Pelletier/Sygma
Back Cover Photograph: Micheline Pelletier/Sygma and Carlos Freire
Typesetting: University of Regina Printing Services, Canada
Production Advisor: Joyce M. Blake
Printed and bound in Canada by: Hignell Printing Limited, Winnipeg

This English language publication would not have been possible without the constant encouragement and support of Marie-Jeanne Bosia-Berberet, President of Soroptimist International, 1993-95.

To Lao, Patchara, Sonta
and all the other "children of Bangkok".

To Margot, my daughter.
To Jean-Paul, my husband.

To Stéphane Thiollier, to his memory.

TABLE OF CONTENTS

Acknowledgements

None of this book, the work with the children of Thailand, the functioning of the project, the investigation and on-the-spot actions, discovery of the refugee camps, trips and long stays in Southeast Asia...even everyday necessities, nothing would have been possible without the work and professional conscience, warmth, faithfulness, trust and friendship of many people. Our sincere thanks go to each and every one of them.

To the *Nouvel Observateur,* without which we, the authors, would never have met in Bangkok.

To the foundation for children, Center for the Protection of Children's Rights, Bangkok (CPCR): Toy, Teelapon, Sanphasit, Païthoon, Bipop, Moo, Poo, Dr. Sem, Dr. Uthai, Mrs. Daeng.

To *Médecins sans Frontières-France*: Dr. Rony Braumann, Dr. Xavier Emmanuelli, Dr. Marc Castellu-Etchegorry, François Dumaine, Dr. Luc Fréjacques and his wife, Jean-Luc Nahel, Anne-Violaine Macon, Michel Fitzbin, Xavier Descarpentiers, Jean-Christophe Rufin, Brigitte Vasset.

To *Médecins sans Frontières-Belgium*: Dr. Reginald Moreels and the Board of Directors. Dr. Jean-Pierre Luxen and his team. Dr. Lydie Van Cauwenberg, Anne Reumont, Olivier Thiteux, Dr. Eric Goemaere, Béatrice Logie, Nadine Van Wallegem, Dr. Myriam Henkens, Mimi Jourdain, Williams Claus, Dr. Paul Gigase, Drs. Patrick and Geneviève Maldague, Marianne Van De Calseyn, Carlos Deboul, Daniel Roland, Annette Bodart, Raymond Philippon, Marc Wolf, Dr. Alain Destexe, Claire Bourgeois, Robert Collart.

To *Médecins sans Frontières-Switzerland*: Paul Vermeulen and the Board of Directors.

Acknowledgements

To François-Xavier Bagnoud: the President Albina Du Bois Rouvray, the Board of Directors: Denis Severis, Georges Casati, Bruno Bagnoud.

To *Terre des Hommes* in Lausanne: Tim Bond.

To the European Community in Brussels and in Bangkok.

To the International Labor Office in Geneva: Carlos Bauverd.

To the Belgium Embassy in Bangkok: Mr. J.-M. Noirfalisse, Ambassador and Ariane Juzen.

To His Majesty King Baudouin of Belgium and Queen Fabiola.

To *France Liberté*: Mrs. Mitterrand and her staff.

To the Foundation Marina Picasso: Marina Picasso and her staff.

To the Delegate General for Children's Rights in Brussels: Claude Lelièvre.

To the *Institute Émile Vandelde*: André Flahout and his staff.

To International Children's Defense in Geneva.

To Parents Anonymous Montreal: Jocelyn Paiement and Celyne Muloin.

To the Association Against Child Prostitution in Paris: Monique Lousteau.

To the Red Cross: ITTRE.

To Saint-Pierre University Hospital in Brussels and the National Office of Birth and Childhood: Prof. Vainsell, Prof. Dachy, Prof. Dopchy, Dr. Levy, Dr. Beeckmans, Dr. Barbara Gevers, Anne-Marie Cauwenberg: "Room 33".

To Attorney Paul Lombart in Paris.

To Sygma: Micheline Pelettier-Decaux and Alain Mingant.

To Interscoop, Paris: Frédéric and Lise Laffont, Sophie and all the staff.

To my friends: Patrick Van De Velde, Georges Ponette, Serge Christians, Marcel Van Erps, Pierre Jambor, Lionel Rosenblatt and Yvette Pierpaoli, Brigitte Maitre, Jeremy Condor, Yvan Sturm, Simone Brocard, Catherine Nickbarte, Yolande and Pierre Goemaere, Marie-Noelle Grell, Anne-Marie Demarbay, Michel Brent, Colette Brackman, Claire Nsen, Béatrice Bracht, Gabrielle de Fierlant Dormer,

Muguette Cozzi, Yvette Hirsch, Francine Versavel, Jacques Vanhee, André Flahaut, Marie-Françoise Lucher-Babel, Nigel Cantwels, Maxime Leforestier, Yohanne Verheyen, Michel Letrowska, Caroline Soupart, Hans Morenhaut, Andrée Despy, Christine Borowiak, Patricia Gandinet, Marie-Françoise Colombani, Georges and Geneviève Deroux, Rosalba Commando, Gilles Cock, Richard Erman, Dominique Gilles, Amélie d'Aultremont, Mrs. Nicoli, Dr. Marcel Germain, Samuel Luret, Ly Sophat, Nacer Leshaef, Marie and Jean Kamps, Charuvan Sursock.

To the service clubs of the city of Nivelles, Soroptimist International Clubs of Geneva, Verviers, Binche, Charleroi, Soleilmont. The White Lotus Foundation of Geneva. The Children's Association of Thailand. The Rotary Clubs of Geneva, Charleroi and Fontaine-Lévêque. The Emile Vandervelde Institute. The Literary Society of Hasselt. The Benge Committee for UNICEF. Cepac Brussels. Fifty-One of Binche and Ohain. The Lions Clubs of Waterloo and Charleroi. Connaissance et Vie. The Kiwanis Club of Charleroi. Marie de Contée. The theatrical group Les Jeunes Planches.

To my family.

Preface

I swear it: I did not want to write this book. I knew what it would mean for me to tell in detail what I saw and lived through during those long years in Thailand. To live it all again, day by day, page by page, the plunge into Bangkok nights, the anguish and wounds of the children, the brutality of the brothel keepers, the quiet cynicism of the pedophiles, the threats of the Chinese Mafia, the horror, the violence, the fear. No, I did not want to descend into this hell again.

I did it because I cannot forget the look in the eyes of Lao, Sonta and Patchara, three little girls, three children among so many others, stolen, kidnapped, beaten and raped in the brothels of Bangkok. We fought to give them their freedom, their childhood. Today, Sonta and Patchara have died of AIDS. And Lao is desperately fighting against the advancement of this disease. Not to talk about them, not to say anything, would mean to send them back to nothingness. I do not have the right.

I produced this book together with Jean-Paul Mari because we conceived it, thought about it and wrote it together, because he saw what I had lived through, he said what he had to say and forced me to share my darkest secrets. But I also did it for selfishness, with the secret hope that at the end of these few hundred pages there would be a sort of exorcism and I would be able to sleep once again without leaving my bedroom light on.

I wrote this book because I promised my Thai friends that I would do it, all the members of the team at the Center for the Protection of Children's Rights, Toy, Teelapon, Pathoon and the others with whom I shared those terrible years. Without them, I would not have been able to do anything. At this moment they are thousands of miles away from me. But I cannot forget what one of them said to me the evening of my departure: "Marie, when you are back in Europe, if you can... help us to continue the fight."

What can I do besides repeat, over and over again, what I saw and learned there, to say that behind the exotic and pleasant facades there

1

are kids who are treated like slaves, who are suffering and who are dying. How many are there? Two hundred thousand out of the eight hundred thousand prostitutes counted in the country? The figures are not easy to establish: the traffic of children is a veritable semi-clandestine market; there is no official information. Of all the child prostitutes we were able to examine, one in four showed signs of abuse, one in four had one or more sexually transmissible diseases, and almost one third was HIV positive.

Also, and above all, I wrote this book to say that the situation is not unchangeable. In four years, the local team at the Center for the Protection of Children's Rights was able to free 1100 children who were locked up in the brothels. And the latest Thai authorities seem to have become more sensitive to the consequences of this scandal.

And finally, I wrote this book to say that we are directly responsible for a part of this trade in children: sixty percent - more than half - of the little prostitutes we questioned have had contact with Western pedophiles. Every month of the year, men buy an airline ticket for Bangkok just to give themselves a few nights with little girls or little boys ten or twelve years old. The same thing that would send them to prison in their own country is worth only a handful of dollars over there. And they know it, they say it, they write it. Best of all, to justify themselves, the pedophiles have elaborated an argument about "new love" mixed with some poor "cultural" excuses and their own kind of so-called truth. The philosophy of "new love" is only a pretext which serves to legitimize a crime. The child prostitutes have given these pedophiles a name: "crocodiles", and they are not wrong.

We met a lot of them. They are not homosexuals, as I often heard it said. Our experience shows that there is no link of cause and effect between homosexuality and pedophilia. The "crocodile" is usually a respected father of a family, a businessman, teacher, worker, architect or nurse, twenty to sixty years old. A commonplace man for a crime that has been made commonplace.

Yes, all of this has to end because it is unbearable and because we can do something about it so that one day it will not be enough to push open the door of a room in a hotel in Bangkok, call the floor boy, give him a few bills and have a child come to your room, the expression of a sleepwalker on his or her face, naked, holding a towel in his or her hand.

Marie-France Botte

1.

BANGKOK : THE PRICE OF A CHILD

Sonta enters the hotel room. Without a word she goes into the bathroom, takes a quick shower and comes back out half naked, a towel around her waist. She doesn't say anything, doesn't seem to see anything, lets the towel drop and lies down on the bed, her eyes fixed on the ceiling, with the tired gestures of an old prostitute. Ready for use. She has the dark skin of the people from the north of Thailand, large brown eyes, and now, an expression of deep anguish. Sonta is just eight years old. A child.

It is 9 P.M. this January 12, 1990. The winter is hot. We are two adults looking at the child in room No. 122 at the Suriwongse Hotel, a brothel in the very center of Bangkok. The room is sordid, with cockroaches running around the bathroom and sheets that smell of mildew. I stand mute, petrified, looking down at the little urchin prostitute who is waiting for us to finish with her. My Thai teammate, Toy, stands on the other side of the bed. Toy, friend, brother, the one who agreed to join me in this interminable investigation about child prostitution in Thailand. He sits down next to the child and talks to her for a long time, in a low voice. At first, the youngster doesn't seem to react. Then she stares at the face of this client who is different from the others. Toy explains to her that nothing is going to happen. Tonight, no one is going to touch her. Abruptly, Sonta relaxes, the tension is gone. She has understood. The little girl picks up the towel and covers herself with a regained sense of modesty. Then, for the first time, she speaks: she's hungry. A dish of fried rice arrives and Toy takes the tray through the half-open door. Above all we must not give the floor boy the impression that we are different from other clients. Sonta digs her hand into the dish of rice and devours it. Tears run down her cheeks. She points to small spots on her arms, back and feet. I have seen marks like these before, dark and round, mostly on the bodies of children who live here, in the bothels. Nasty cigarette burns, like those sometimes seen on the bodies of abused children who are brought to the emergency rooms of European hospitals. Sonta moans. Her back is drenched with sweat, a thick, green liquid seeps from an infected sore: this child is sick.

The room is cool, the air conditioner is the only luxury. Over the bed, the mirror is greasy and two used condoms lie limp in the ashtray. I don't like this mirror. I imagine a hidden eye evily watching us from the other side, waiting patiently for us to make an error; that would be the end of us.

Now Sonta is talking, but what she says is confused. She has lost the notion of time, mixes the past and present. She is completely lost. Twenty-four hours a day, her body is at the disposal of others. Toy gently questions her in Thai. What kind of person was the last adult she met? Where? What was he like? What did he ask her to do? Sonta tells him. It was just 3 o'clock, in room 147: a big man, white skin, waiting, lying on the bed. Sonta takes a shower. He watches her, seems to be impatient. A bottle of whiskey and two glasses are on the only table. The room reeks of tobacco and alcohol. She lies on the bed, the man and his 200 pounds immobilize her. He kisses her, fondles her, then the client demands fellatio: the child does it. Her mouth, too small, covered with absesses, is painful... Toy translates word for word, her narration becomes unbearable. But we must continue. After a few minutes in the room, the man frees the child and rings for the floor boy. They argue, louder and louder. Sonta cannot understand but she sees that the man is not smiling and that the floor boy keeps throwing her black looks. An unsatisfied client is a lost client. She knows she will be beaten.

The floor boy takes the little girl back to her prison, a locked garage guarded by an armed guard and a rigid old Chinese woman. The floor boy growls: Sonta works badly, she doesn't smile and the customers complain. The blows begin to rain on her. Five children sitting on straw mats watch the scene. They, too, pass their time in this room fifteen by eighteen feet, waiting to be called. On the upper floors, other children are already occupied. At eight years old, Sonta is the youngest, and yet she is the oldest. The blows continue to fall until she collapses.

Now the child is worn out and the room is silent once again. I have a lump in my throat, Toy cannot speak, Sonta cries. Toy, usually so strong, turns his face away and goes to the window. A few hundred yards away, life continues in the Patpong quarter, its bars crammed with tourists and whores.

Everything on the street is lit up, small restaurants wait for customers. Alone, at the edge of the sidewalk, a big, fat man gulps some soup. What if he were Sonta's last customer, the one from room 147? Absurd. Farther along, a foreign couple stops to bargain for a T-shirt, go on, pass an adolescent of less than fifteen who is looking for a customer with the eye and allure of a street broad.

Toy's expression is lost, far away, very far from the theater of the street. Sonta turns on the television and stares at the screen where temples are being shown to traditional Thai music in the backround. Bonzes offer presents to a giant Buddah. Hah! The hotel also has a religious altar. Opposite the reception, a wooden house called "spiritual house" waits for offerings. Sonta remembers: her village, the red soil of the Gold Triangle on the border shared by three countries, the women with their backs bent in the rice paddies and her family, which belongs to the Akas tribe, nomads. A hard life where there is no school but with children's laughter and rice every day. Sonta also remembers that day in April 1989, the minibus that came down the dirt road, a woman wearing a green dress, her hair in a chignon and graceful hands. An elegant and beautiful woman, so beautiful! And the red and yellow balloons she gave out! The little girl approached the vehicle and... Afterward, everything went very fast. The screams, the wad of cotton over her mouth, the deep sleep, the arrival in Bangkok, the unknown megalopolis, stopping at the Suriwongse Hotel and, immediately, the first customer. She remembers trying to defend herself, the man she bit, and then the blows, blows and more blows that crush all resistance. And after?... Silence. Sonta has had enough. And so have we. It's midnight. She sinks into a deep sleep. Toy covers her with the bedsheet, a piece of gray, worn out cloth that makes the child look like a small dead corpse. Oddly, I think of my grandmother, an old lady of ninety, coiled up on her sofa in Brussels. I search my memory for her odor of grandmother, the taste of her pies, the sound of her voice... Ah! Grandmother and her eternal advice. Grandmother Simm, my thoughts turn toward you to find the strength to not accept what I have seen, to not forget what I have heard.

What time is it? I don't know. Toy is stretched out on the bed, the television crackles its last Thai news bulletin. Our eyes remain wide open. Our looks are glued to Sonta. Toy's hand is resting on my shoulder and I don't have the strength to say a word. It is already too late to draw back. My memories are sullied. I know that I will not come out of this mission unscathed.

Five o'clock: Toy hurls himself out of the bed, we're both standing, distraught. A man knocks on the door of the room with incredible violence. I'm petrified with fear. Sonta has understood. Like a robot she walks toward the door but Toy has already opened the door and blocked the child's way. The floor boy is there, rigid, a hard look on his face and his hand stretched out. He wants five hundred bahts more to finish the night. Pay cash or he will take the child; someone else is waiting for her in another room. We pay. Sonta buries herself under the sheet. Her sobs fill the room. Only the night is left.

In the morning, we have to leave the room and give the little girl back. We search for words, motions. In vain. There are no words when a child is abandoned. We feel filthy dirty. It is breakfast time and the restaurant is full of male tourists. I flee.

A few months later, we are back at the Suriwongse Hotel. This time we have come to find Sonta. More than a month has passed since we lived through that night, forty days of looking for child prostitutes in brothels and on the streets, forty breakfasts in brothels face to face with a very particular kind of tourist. We must recognize that we are physically exhausted, morally worn out. Falling asleep has become more and more difficult. Maybe that is why, for the first time, we are going to break the code of security that we had established from the beginning. Simple rules: first of all, never go back to see a child. And above all, never attempt to free her. I was the one who broke. Toy resisted for a long time; I insisted, stubborn, reasoning, playing on emotions, sometimes sweet, sometimes agressive, threatening to act alone... Toy ended up giving in, accepting to attempt a rescue. Only one. And now I am scared to death.

For the hundredth time we cross Patpong, one of the hot districts of Bangkok. Deep down inside, I hope that Sonta is no longer at the Suriwongse. But nothing has changed. The fat Chinese is still sitting on his chair behind the counter and four clients are watching a porno video. The floor boy hands us the key to room No. 138, smaller, more dismal than the first one and teaming with cockroaches. Disappointment: two clients have already paid cash and the little girl is working in another room. Impossible to hire Sonta this evening. To replace her, the floor boy proposes two little boys ten and eleven years old as well as a little Chinese girl. Toy insists. We want Sonta. Impossible. The clients payed a very high price, he cannot go back on his agreement. For this evening, failure.

The next day we are back again and Sonta finally comes to the room. Without a glance, she goes into the bathroom. I can hardly recognize her. She is thiner and seems exhausted. Her body is covered with small dark blotches. But above all, her face has lost all expression. Toy asks her to sit down, but the child remains standing at the foot of the bed, her look somewhere else, lost in another world. Finally, she lies down but stays hopelessly mute. The hours pass. The night is long and we turn on the television to cover the sound of our voices. The child has not raised her head. We must save Sonta, steal her, get her out of here. This child is going to die at the feet of the next client. And we will not have tried to do anything to save her! We have to steal her. Toy is furious. He knows it is too risky. We don't have the least chance of getting out of here. There's the floor boy, the child's unpredictable attitude, the hotel's hostile clients who may even be accomplices, the receptionist downstairs, the street... Toy's arguments ring in my head and yet I know that it will be impossible for us to live if we abandon Sonta again. I am not a believer, I have no God to whom I can entrust the child, to whom I can hang on to. What will be left? Just the image of Sonta and of our cowardice. There is no question about it, there is only one chance: buy the child from the old Chinese at the entrance. Toy rejects the idea. Perhaps he and I have come to the parting of the ways; the idea of being left alone freezes my blood. Finally, Toy reluctantly accepts the idea of buying Sonta. He does not agree, but he cannot resign himself to abandoning me. Good.

I order a gin and orange and try to concentrate on the scenario. I can imagine the Chinese man's reaction. I count the money we have left: two thousand dollars and a little more than ten thousand francs. It should be enough. The child is sick, she will probably bring in less money to the manager of this brothel; it's a point of argument. He'll accept, he has to accept! Toy sits on the chair, despondent. His gaze rests now on Sonta, now on me. His big black eyes betray him, the situation eludes him. It's daytime now. From the street the noise of cars and the cries of peddlers can be heard through the window. It's time. Sonta is still lying on the bed. I go out. In the hall I pass a tired client who smells of alcohol. I pass by the floor boy sleeping on a chair in the corner by the stairs. My knees are shaking with fear, but something forces me to go on. The ground floor is nearly empty, a client is sleeping on his seat and the porno video is still running. Sitting on his chair, the fat Chinese is counting his money, several thousand bahts lay in bundles on the counter. He raises an eye and stares at me. Five or six yards separate us. There is no turning back. I tell him my arguments: I love children, particularly Sonta; I have moved to Bangkok for a year or two, this little girl is nice and I am willing to take her... He doesn't blink an eye. I let it fall: "Your price is my price." His eyes light up and the discussion begins. The floor boy has arrived and the two men talk in Thai. Above all, don't show how afraid I am, my efforts to swallow my saliva, my hands dripping with sweat. An eternity later, the mouth of the Chinese becomes round with a figure: "Eight hundred dollars. No less." I dig my hand into my bag. He turns his back to me and counts. I climb the stairs and go back to the room. In two words I explain the situation to Toy; we grab our bags and the child. Sonta lets me dress her, her look always absent. I take her by the hand and cross the hall toward the entrance. The client is still sleeping, the video blasts an infernal music and the Chinese watches us pass. Outside Toy hurries us along. We walk in a frenzy. A taxi passes nearby, Toy signals it to stop. Suddenly I am overcome with doubt. Everything is going too fast! We are going to be accused of kidnapping. About-face! I go back to the Suriwongse. The Chinese is still there, sitting on his high chair. I explain again, almost brutally: "We are leaving with the girl. And we will not come back. Do you understand?" The man slowly lifts his head, looks at me and bites off his words: "You have bought her. Now, clear off." I turn my back on him. His words ring in my head. For less than five thousand francs, eight hundred dollars, we have bought a child.

I feel dizzy. Grandmother, tell me that all of this is only the nightmare of a little blonde girl who stuffed herself on too much chocolate. Tell me, what am I doing here thousands of miles from Brussels? How is it possible, in just a few years, the time of a breath in memory, to go from a big cosy house to the cold corridors of a hospital in Belgium and then find myself, on a tropical winter night, in a brothel on the other side of the world bargaining for the salvation of a broken doll? When did all of this really begin? Maybe it was the day I decided to look for those children who disappeared from the refugee camps in the North of Thailand. Or a few weeks ago when I pushed open the door of a humanitarian organization. Or again, that mean winter day in Europe, cold and rainy, when three phantoms broke into my very well-ordered life. That was five years ago. Go back...

2.

BRUSSELS, SAINT PETER'S HOSPITAL
SATURDAY, NOVEMBER 20, 1985
SEVEN A.M.

The hospital corridor is empty. An elderly man dressed in hospital pajamas patiently waits for the coffee machine to drop his plastic cup. He has a sad air about him. I linger a moment before taking the elevator. It has been more than two years since I started working as a social assistant in this hospital in the center of town, the underprivileged quarter of Brussels. The building is old, rotting. At night the long corridors seem endless. The hospital is antiquated but full of charm, perhaps because of the thousands of people who have left a piece of their lives here, their hopes and their revival. Like thumbing its nose at the dark. This morning the sixth floor psychiatric ward is still deserted.

First cup of coffee, first file; Marianne's file is still open on my desk. I put it away automatically and think about her daughter, Rouquine, a two-year-old child that I see every week. Marianne is twenty years old and prostitutes herself to survive. We have known each other for several months now. Marianne comes for psychological therapy and hospitalizes her daughter each time she is depressed. Rouquine has always been poorly taken care of, but the mother/child relationship continues to be excellent. And Marianne has promised to protect her child from now on. She has agreed to leave the little girl in the hospital eight hours a day. When the mother is in crisis, the child is hospitalized. Room No. 33 of the pediatric ward has become her second family. Sometimes Marianne can make herself deaf to all arguments; she screams, attacks everyone within her reach. At these times she shouts that she is a prostitute, takes mean pleasure in scaring the people in the waiting room, provokes them, yelling that she rounds off her income from Welfare with passers-by at fifty francs. Marianne is in distress.

Second cup of coffee. It was a bad night. Philippe, my boyfriend, left me; it was quite a blow. Especially since he works in the same hospital. Forget it. My beeper rings; this little magic box is the line that attaches all of us to the life of this enormous machine, the university hospital. This time there is a message from my father. During the last several weeks he has gotten very thin and has trouble breathing. He is nervous and has called to remind me that yesterday evening he asked me to make an appointment with a specialist in respiratory illnesses. I go down to the third floor and reserve Monday morning to take him to a specialist. I don't think it will be very serious; he is still in good shape and very active as usual. The morning passes quickly. A new two-month old child is waiting in pediatrics: a simple arm fracture. But the baby's parents are bizarre and the pediatrician would like to get a clearer picture of the situation. The infant will be hospitalized long enough to understand what really happened. Routine.

Monday, 8 o'clock a.m. I have breakfast with my father just before his medical examination. He eats a croissant, jokes, tells a story to hide his nervousness, asks where I am moving - four trunks in all! - and describes his latest car, an English sports model. It's time; we climb the stairs directly to radiology. The minute the x-rays are finished, my father is already in the hallway. He smiles: "It went fine." I knock on the door of the laboratory. Inside, a doctor is holding the x-rays and dictating the results to a secretary. He notes my white coat and hands me the file: "Your patient can live two months more. Cancer. There is metastasis everywhere."

What did he say? My legs wobble, my knees buckle, I find myself on the floor. My patient... My father... Two months at the most... The doctor bends over me, looks at the name written on my coat and the name on the file. He understands: "Shit! His daughter...She's his daughter!" I am finally able to get up and, dazed, pick up the file. Words well up from my throat: "I hate you! All of you! I hate you!" Outside, I get myself back together. Above all, don't let on to my father. I smile and take him toward the exit. My father walks slowly; the corridor never ends and in my head, a voice hammers away: "Two months. Just two months. Two months at the most." My father dies forty days later.

Anguish always comes with the night. This Friday in February the nurses are putting the sick children to sleep. The siren of an ambulance can be heard at the emergency entrance. I am tired and it is too late to join my friends. The hospital consumes all my life. It is a twenty minute walk to my house; the cat is waiting on the doorstep, the answering machine gives its messages: nothing urgent. I fall asleep. When the telephone rings, the digital clock indicates five o'clock in the morning. On the phone, Barbara, a pediatrician I often work with, speaks in a tense voice, "Hello, listen, it's about your little patient, Rouquine. The police have brought her to emergency. You had better come right away." At the hospital, the waiting room is full to bursting, children are crying, parents are getting impatient and the nurses are trying to smile at everyone. Rouquine is there, sitting on the examining table, her eyes red from tears, a rubber giraffe in her hand. Beside her, a policeman on duty waits, a file resting on his knees. Rouquine gobbles down a bottle of baby formula offered to her by a student nurse. The policeman takes me to an office and tells me what happened: at No. 112 Verte Street where Marianne lives, a flood of water came through the ceiling of the apartments below. Rouquine was heard crying on the second floor. The neighbor climbed the stairs and pushed open the door of the two-room apartment. Rouquine was sitting in her baby chair, alone. In the bathroom, Marianne was dead. Strangled.

In a few years, living with a foster family, Rouquine will become a little girl with big brown eyes and carrot colored hair, playing at the playground like thousands of other kids her age. But for the moment Rouquine is in a hospital bed sleeping, an orphan at two. Outside, day has come. It is raining in Brussels. Now, three phantoms haunt my life at the hospital: my father, Philippe and Marianne.

On the sixth floor, in the psychiatric ward, life continues. My colleague is beginning her tenth year of work; children pass every day and I try to block out my feelings, to remain technical. My work has become a matter of "earning my daily bread." I am filled with doubt. I cannot stay here any longer, I don't want to any more. There must be life somewhere else. My family and my friends do not understand me; they talk about escape, about the beginning of depression. I really don't feel sad, I just want to try something else, to change my life, not to bungle it. Go! Good bye Brussels.

Chance does not exist. A friend speaks to me about a small French organization that is looking for someone to work in a refugee camp in Thailand. It is hard to get to Paris: France is paralyzed by a transportation strike. It takes me twelve hours to reach the French capital, but one afternoon is enough to convince the president to hire me. The organization is too family-like to be really professional. More annoying, the job they offer me is not clear - the teaching of French and "socialization" to Cambodian children in difficulty in a refugee camp one hundred miles from Bangkok. It doesn't matter! I decide to go and sign the contract the same day. On the train back to Brussels I fall asleep easily, convinced that I have made the right decision. All I have to do now is say goodbye to my family, my friends... and Jean-Paul for six months. I met Jean-Paul a few months ago, after my break-up with Philippe. Since then we have practically spent all our week-ends together. He knows everything, everyone, the places that are the most 'in' at the moment, the latest exposition and the latest book. His energy and his knowledge charm me. I am going to miss him. However, my decision is made. In my suitcase: *Le Petite Prince,* by Saint-Exupéry, some photographs, personal effects, just twenty-six pounds of luggage. On the evening of my departure, Jean-Paul is sad. Perhaps I am leaving just at the moment when everything could change. But it is too soon, the phantoms still haunt me and it will take time to get rid of them. How could I know that later, much later, the man I was leaving behind me would become my husband and the adoptive father of a Vietnamese baby that we would choose together in Hanoi? How could I imagine that he would remain in my life, often thousands of miles away from me, but always so close? That nothing would be possible without his support, his understanding, his strength?

Right now I know none of this. My departure is for tomorrow. I am going.

3.

THAILAND: THE PAPER HAND PUPPETS
OF PHANAT-NIKOM CAMP

Bangkok Airport: the air is hot and humid and my clothes stick to my skin after twelve hours of flying time. The center of town is one hour away by taxi, traffic is dense, the main road is lined with buildings under construction and shanty towns are pressed right up to the railroad tracks. People live here like ants and the least little space is made to pay. The agreed meeting place is a small gray hotel wedged between two abandoned buildings and a mosque close to the French Embassy. A volunteer from the Association should have left a "pass" there for me, an indispensable document to get into the camp, as well as a map showing me how to get to Phanat-Nikom City. At the hotel, however, no document is waiting for me. Mystery. I use this wasted day to wander through the streets of the old Chinese quarter. I enter a pagoda; it is all red and gold. A traditional pharmacy, set up in the courtyard, offers buffalo horn, snake scales and other strange drugs, elixirs of happiness. A very old Chinese woman weighs a block of white chalk, covers her cheeks with it and, obviously satisfied, negotiates her price. A little girl is sitting on the wooden counter swinging her legs; she looks at my pale blond hair out of the corner of her eye. Further along, a shop sells shirts, trousers and hats: clothes made out of paper to dress the deceased, new clothes for a new life. Here, the business of death takes on an allure of coquetry. Night has come in just a few moments, thick clouds of gas fumes catch at my throat and clusters of people hang on to busses filled to bursting. Children dressed in pajamas play on the sidewalks, and soup vendors begin their rounds. You can get lost in Bangkok, the maze of its tiny streets, the mixture of its odors: ginger, incense and garbage. At the hotel, the dining room is deserted. I am not hungry and go to bed without opening my suitcase.

Six thirty a.m. : the noise of the *touk-touks* reaches up to the third floor. These small motorized tricycles zip across the city, a tank of gas on the passenger seat; the drivers are intoxicated fifteen hours a day at the wheel of these bombs on wheels. There is finally a message for me at the reception: a local bus leaves for Phanat-Nikom at 11 o'clock.

The bus station is awesome. Lines of busses are waiting for passengers, hundreds of Asians push to buy tickets. Near me a young Thai about fifteen has raided a shop and in a plastic bag carries a cupboardful of food. Departure at nine o'clock on the non-stop bus. "Tamada" is stamped on the ticket, a term used for vehicles without air conditioning. I get on bus No. 4 and take seat No. 22. The driver finishes adjusting the video and the title promises a film of kung-fu, violence and red corpuscles guaranteed. Three hours later the countryside becomes yellow with vegetation burned by a dry season that has been too long. In the fields, women carry drums of water balanced on their backs: farmers irrigate the rice paddy fields any way they can! Children in blue and white uniforms walk in single file on the edge of the road carrying tin billycans in their hands. In the distance, a temple and a school can be seen.

At the station of Phanat-Nikom in the public square; George is there holding a piece of cardboard with my name on it. George has been working six months at the school; the former student of oriental languages in Paris has chosen to come here to practice his Thai. He gives me some information and the key to a house which four of us will share. Work begins tomorrow. As soon as the presentations are over, George turns on his heel. This man is rather cold; I am left alone. I decide to borrow the watchman's bicycle to visit the neighborhood where everyone is already in nightclothes. Nothing is missing except a nightcap, but we are far away from northern Europe. There are eating-houses everywhere and the smell of food simmering on old stoves is a delight. I stop at a diner where the whole family is working in the kitchen. A grandmother, staring fixedly, fiddles with a jade bracelet while she hums a Chinese song. Koon Maie is one hundred and two years old and she is blind. A little girl touches her wrinkled hands and places a porcelain bowl full of boiling-hot noodle soup in front of her. Life in Phanat-Nikom could be summed up in these few winding streets around the market. People go to bed early here.

I leave for the camp at six-thirty the next morning. At the end of the road there are two police blocks, long rolls of barbed wire and a main entrance guarded by armed soldiers; this refugee camp resembles a prison camp. It is divided into two separate sections by the road: to the left, the refugees who are awaiting departure to foreign countries, mainly Cambodians and Laotians; to the right, thousands of Vietnamese, those who didn't make it. They will never leave. We enter the fenced-in area. A soldier carefully verifies each authorization. Strangely, he holds the document upside down. The school consists of wooden pavilions with sheet metal roofs; in front of each one, children and adults wait patiently. George and Virginia lead me toward the last building, the class for the smallest. Virginia is a teacher and has been responsible for the older children for almost a year. She speaks to me at length about the thirty-odd brown heads which will be mine daily. There are no chairs in the classroom, just a table, a large blackboard and large straw mats covering the ground. The walls are empty, we will have to give them a little life. The children introduce themselves one after the other and observe me covertly. How am I going to remember all these difficult names: Sovatana, Bounsri, Sophalè, Arine, Sophat, Ratana...? All these kids were born in border camps after their parents arrived in Thai territory. Three little girls arrived late in 1984; three sisters, seven, nine and eleven years old; three orphans. The mother accompanying them is dead, killed by Khmer Rouge soldiers. The little girls were picked up less than a half mile from the border. I glance at their card, which mentions behavioral problems and depression of the two youngest. Sophat, the oldest, has assumed responsibility of the family. The three of them crouch together at the back of the class: "Those three are inseparable," says Virginia. They live five yards from the school in "House 34 C", the wood and straw building shared with nine other refugees whose presence guarantees the children's security.

Mrs. Surin, a woman of 40, a volunteer teacher at the school, invites me to share her lunch. She once taught French at the high school of Phnom Penh in Cambodia. "The good old days," she says. In 1970, Mrs. Surin married a professor of law and gave birth to her first baby right away. Five years later, Pol Pot swept everything away in the name of Communism. Today there is nothing left of Mrs. Surin's happiness: her husband was struck to death with an ax on the side of Highway 3, her child died of hunger a few months later, her parents and cousins are dead, killed or consumed by sickness. She fled by foot to the border. For twenty-three days she walked in the forest among bodies mutilated by mines, corpses that would rot on the ground. Each step was a challenge to the enemy's traps. Old people and very small children, exhausted, had to be abandoned. Thousands of lives ended there, along the winding pathway, at the foot of an unknown tree, in the bushes at the end of the world. Seeing them, men and women would look the other way as they passed. "We didn't have any choice," recalls Mrs. Surin. A million people had to pay for this insanity with their lives, more than two hundred fifty thousand to wait in the camps of Southeast Asia for a door to finally open, a door to a third country. Third? The first is the country of their roots, their memories; the second is the country of exile and waiting; the third is the country of dreams and hope. The country that many will never reach. When the waiting becomes too humiliating, it can happen that a refugee chooses a fourth country, within reach of his desperation: a corner of the camp, away from stares, with a tree to hang himself. Mrs. Surin gets up, embarrassed, excusing herself a thousand times for telling this story: "You understand, I cannot forget. I cannot..." On the table, our soup remains cold and untouched. It is two o'clock, time to go back to class.

The first exhausting week ends. Six straight days, from six-thirty a.m. to six-thirty p.m., the sun beating down on our heads, our feet in thick dust. The roof of the classes is made of sheet metal, and some afternoons the thermometer reaches 100° F regardless of the tired fan which only stirs the hot air. But I don't feel the fatigue too much; the children are bursting with energy, they are hungry for knowledge and even the shyest begin to speak. When we mention Cambodia, however, they withdraw into silence. Total refusal, even to the point of becoming aggressive. We must go beyond, break down the walls of this prison within them that is suffocating them. An idea! We can make papier-mâché puppets; each child will be represented by a figurine that he will animate himself. The children are enthusiastic and want to begin immediately. Pans are found and filled with paper to soak overnight. A hubbub fills the class and each child imagines his character. The girls go to look for scraps of cloth to make sarongs, a length of traditional cloth worn around the waist. The choice is precise: it determines the status of a woman. The work is interrupted by the bell; the children scramble toward the door. A normal scene if we forget the barbed wire.

The next morning Chanta comes to my office early. He is dragging as usual, pretending he has lost his notebook or has a stomach ache. His problem is something else: Chanta lives alone with a handicapped, embittered father. He has no one to notice that his T-shirt is too small, to console him, to cuddle him. Sometimes this little man hangs around on the school patio until six o'clock and, with a sad face, watches us leave. I usually meet his father when I accompany the boy to building No. 12; the twenty square yards they live in are indescribably untidy. How can I reproach him. He is an old soldier of the opposition forces to the regime; battles and mines have taken their toll: he has lost a leg. The humanitarian organization, Handicap International, has made him a wooden prosthesis which allows him to get around more easily. But the wound is deeper. Day and night this forty-year-old man broods about his past, his dead wife, the tragedy of his whole family. Their departure for France is scheduled for next month. His wife's uncle is a jeweler and has obtained 'family re-grouping'. Finally, a little luck. Even so, it is not easy to leave Asia. Here, ties to the ancestral birthplace are still very important. Leaving is resented as downright abandonment of the others, both the living and the dead. And Chanta's father never ceases to recall those thousands of souls that wander around in the Cambodian capital, those corpses thrown into pits without a burial who will never be able to find rest. A few years ago, his wife, close to Cambodian high society, was still teaching dancing at the royal palace. The family enjoyed a peaceful existence. Twelve years later, lost in a camp with twenty thousand refugees, a father in exile drags his stump around looking for a meaning to his life.

Two months have passed since my arrival; the Chinese grocers have found me lodging and I am going to move this evening. A corner all to myself. At last! Mr. Hoa's house is lost in the jungle of a garden. Behind a door of sheet metal, a short walkway leads to four wooden walls, rice straw and a roof. A doll house. Mr. Hoa, an old man, lives alone since his wife died. Fifteen or twenty cats have made this their home and reign over the four-room house. I rent the top floor and the terrace from where the view of surrounding vegetation is impenetrable. The bathroom is located at the far end of the garden and the electricity does not always work, but a small bulb will be enough. I relish the idea of living alone again; I have already adopted the place. When I return from school in the evenings, Mr. Hoa comes to sit on the terrace. He gets excited, talks in Chinese without stopping so I can't understand a word he's saying. So what! Mr. Hoa can talk for hours and is content with a smile and a kind ear. Our living together is a big story. My presence

seems to articulate his life.   He watches me intently and waits until
evening to takes advantage of the least opportunity to run off with my
bike.   Our days begin at five thirty when the smoke from his so-called
stove fills my room, a smell of coffee and burning that makes me feel
sick.   How can I explain to Grandfather Hoa that Sunday is a day when
we can sleep late and that it is useless to rant and rave to make me get up?
On weekends I search the market or write letters for hours.   My wish to
share everything I see is so great that I swamp my friends and family with
letters.   Stopping at the mailbox on my way home is very important.
Sometimes it is empty and the night is long.   But very often the days are
colored with aerograms, those small blue envelopes sent by air mail.
Jean-Paul stays up at night to write me; his letters are a breath of oxygen.
All the more so because days at the camp are becoming more and more
difficult; refugees are being repatriated in secret on orders from the Thai
army;   people are afraid, and as the hour for us to leave the camp
approaches, at sunset, we can feel everyone getting panicky . We do not
have the right to stay in the camp after six-thirty p.m.   At night and on
weekends the refugees are at the mercy of the Thai soldiers.   The soldiers
regularly enter homes and confiscate the papers issued to refugees by the
High Commissioner.   This crumpled, crushed piece of paper indicates the
reference number and route of every individual.   It allows a refugee to get
rations of rice and dried fish and to receive health care at the camp
hospital.   This document is all the fortune a refugee has: his identity.
Mrs. Surin hides it in a worn plastic envelope which she keeps under her
mat at night.   When the soldiers ask her for her paper, she always says
she left it at the French school.   "I am not afraid," our teacher says
quietly.   "I have already lost everything."   Others crack under the menace;
they are stripped of their rice ration for the week or of a last piece of
jewelry.   Sometimes a woman is taken to an empty building and the
soldiers rape her.   In the morning, the people of the quarter speak only in
half words.   The victim, the woman, withdraws into her own silence for
fear of retaliation and nights to come.   Whenever a representative of some
organization raises this question, the authorities merely deny it.

The plight of the Vietnamese is the most tragic; the Thai foster a deep
and historic hatred toward them.   The fact is they fear them.   And
therefore they hound them fiercely.   Children continue to arrive every
week in 'nutshells', boats of human beings tossed around in the sea for
ten or fifteen days, surviving storms, hunger, thirst, Thai pirate attacks,
rape and torture.   Survivors.   Often a family from Saigon will sell its

home and all its jewelry to buy the right to embark an eleven-year-old child. If the child survives the crossing, as soon as he reaches the camp he immediately declares that he is an orphan and tries to get sent to the United States. There, once he is settled with a family in Chicago or Denver, the remaining children and family in Vietnam have only to ask for family re-grouping. Deception of the adoptive family and anger of the American Secretary of Foreign Affairs! As a result, the preliminary examination of these cases is always difficult. The child knows very well that he is gambling the future of his whole family in three interviews. I have seen children act out ingenious scenarios and succeed in tricking the embassy officials even though the information attached to the file tells of the existence of a family of twelve in Vietnam. Blessed kids!

But most often the attempts fail. Desperation, suicides and violence are the daily lot of the rare teams that work here. The camp commander, a man of about fifty, pushes perversion to the point of solemnly organizing departures for the airport in the court next to section 'C'. Clusters of men, women and children then start pushing against the link fencing that separates them from a dream. I detest this moment, torn between the joy of the families that are finally leaving the camp after several years of exile and the sight of those left behind for nothing.

The life I lead in this camp of refugees is bizarre: there are no bounds to the joy and sorrow, justice and injustice. Not a day passes that some incident does not force me to reflect. I naively discover that every man is capable of the worst and of the best. Here, destiny has brought together victims of authoritarian regimes and volunteers who, believe it or not, offer their time, sometimes their lives, to the refugees side by side with the Thai soldiers who trample on human rights. We live and work in this barbed wire enclosure; at mealtime we eat the same soup. The confusion and doubt that fill me on certain nights seems normal to me, but my colleagues think that it is useless to ask themselves this kind of question. What? It is enough to be here. That's all! But I cannot; I need to understand.

Today the children act out another play. We have prepared a small stage for the game with the hand puppets. One difficult situation follows another: we have to imagine Ratana lost in Paris, Chanta blocked in a phone booth in the Place de la Republique, and Chem being chased by a ferocious dog. The puppets seem almost alive and right from the start the children laugh as they have never laughed before. Spectators - children and adults - crowd around the windows. We have our audience; it is a real performance.

The rainy season has begun and tons of water pour on the camp every day. We walk in the mud and when the storm breaks around three o'clock in the afternoon, the rain beats so hard on the metal roof it is impossible to hear in the classroom. At Mr. Hoa's house, we set buckets around because the roof is leaking here and there. I love these rainy evenings that are cool as the night and the beat of the rain that lulls you to sleep. Tomorrow, Friday, is an important date: I have been here six months! Time passes... This morning the entrance to the camp is blocked and we have to wait twenty minutes before we can reach the school building. Sovatana, a pupil, rushes into the class and, in a complete state of confusion, tells a story of soldiers, families and small pieces of paper. A third of the children are not present for roll call. I look for Mrs. Surin. She is the only one who can help me to unravel this story.

Sovatana tries again to tell her story from the beginning: soldiers came into homes at dusk confiscating the refugees' papers, then they left, taking several families with them. The little girl continues: people were screaming, crying, soldiers pushing them, the group disappeared swallowed up by the black night. At dawn a bus passes in front of the camp. It is taking the refugees to a camp at the border. Passengers throw paper butterflies from the windows on which they have written their registration number. Calls for help. Sovatana followed the bus as far as the gate and picked up the little pieces of papers. She reads us every message, then she sits down, puts her head in her hands and cries. I cannot help remembering Grandmother Simm's stories: the Second World War, trains full of Jews leaving the city of Malines in Belgium to go to the death camps, and the messages thrown from openings in the freight cars; pieces of paper, with a name, a number, borne by the wind.

We get out our papier-mâché puppets, but nine of them remain in the bottom of the box. The children use their characters to tell what they saw. Everything is anguish and fear. Sovatana throws her puppet against the wall and leaves the class without a word. Many of the puppets land in a corner of the room. Chanta tears up her figurine's costume piece by piece. They all leave. Alone in the classroom, I pick up the pieces of paper and cloth. I could not hope for anything better to exorcise the demons. I cry as I rearrange the puppets in the box.

Mrs. Surin comes in, sits down and looks at me: "Do you want to leave?" Leave? I dry my tears; I don't know, perhaps. In the office of the camp commander, the officer explains that the "displaced" refugees were refused by a possible welcoming country. These expeditious measures are not the first here. It does not matter that the refugees have been through ten years of humiliation and camp. There are no human rights for people on the register who have been refused by an international organization. In an office somewhere in the West, a man crossed out nine names, and in Bangkok an officer confirmed the order for transfer. They administer papers, not men. For me to stay here would mean to support this kind of procedure. My decision is made, I will go back to Europe.

Three weeks remain till the day of my departure and Mr. Hoa has trouble accepting this news. Something has faded from his gaze. His life has come to revolve around mine, his day follows the rhythm of my hours; perhaps the idea of being alone again is unbearable to him. Poor Mr. Hoa. A going away party is prepared at school on Wednesday. The children decorate the class, they go through their dance steps and one by one bring their drawings to my work table; this is my last day in the camp. I look at each face intently and try to fix them all in my memory, to retain the odors. My fingers caress Chanta's head. A little girl comes up and gives me the carton of puppets. They are all there, in the bottom of the box. During the performances, the puppets personified the life of each child. I will take them with me so that I will never forget.

Behind the barbed wire of the main entrance to Phanat-Nikom camp hands are waving, children are screaming. Mrs. Surin grasps my hands and says in her sweet musical voice, "Leave quickly, but don't abandon us." Chanta's father shouts; a phrase reaches me, "See you soon, in France!"

In the car, sitting beside the driver, I see the green rice paddies; the farmers with their curved backs stream by for the last time. I don't dare look back as we pass the barrier leaving the camp for fear that I will not be able to leave any more. At the bus station, I catch sight of Mr. Hoa, his body broken by his great age, watching the passenger entrance. He is holding a gray paper bag in his left hand and lets out a cry when he sees me approach the ticket counter. He laughs, says a phrase in Chinese. I have the impression that I understand. His eyes are red. He gives me his package and disappears without a word. Goodbye, Mr. Hoa. I left some small gifts for you hidden in our house: French cigarettes, a small bottle of "Mékong" liquor, a 20 lb. bag of rice hidden behind the door of my room and the equivalent of two months' rent on the small table.

It is a one-hundred mile bus ride to Bangkok. In twenty-four hours I will be back in my country. The six months I lived at Phanat-Nikom pass slowly through my mind. I don't regret anything. I learned a lot with the refugees;   I shared terrible moments of discouragement, but also moments of laughter, of trust. I loved them. There is still one question that pounds in my head: what happens to the children who disappear from the camps?

4.

THE BEGINNING OF A TRAIL

In Brussels, disappointment awaits me: no one is interested in the two hundred and fifty thousand Cambodian exiles in Thailand. My friends are worried about their own daily problems: taxes or the new apartment to move into. Only Jean-Paul shows any real interest in these people on the other side of the world. He is getting ready to leave Brussels to go back to Nairobi for the United Nations. We have only three weeks until the day of his departure and we share every minute we have left.

Passing through Geneva to visit some friends, a poster about the organization *Terre des Hommes* catches my eye. Lausanne is not far away; I run. Their offices are located on Mont-sur-Lausanne. The person responsible for recruitment makes me several offers: a mission in Taiwan where little girls are caught in the network of prostitution, a position as coordinator in Egypt, or a mission in Thailand for refugee children. Luckily the three Program Directors are abroad, which gives me the time to reflect.

Back in Brussels my heart wavers between the Middle East and Asia. This morning a telephone call from Tim perturbs my reflection. Tim is responsible for the Asian sector of *Terre des Hommes*. He is terribly British, six feet tall, blue eyes, likes gin and curried foods, and reads the *Herald Tribune*. Above all, he is an uncontested specialist on the problem of street children whether in Bogota, Delhi, Katmandu or Dacca. He is a courageous man who was deported from Thailand for having accused the authorities of collaborating with the networks of child prostitution. He has just come back from a mission and hopes that we can meet as soon as possible to talk about the program in Taiwan. My intuition tells me that this mission is not for me. I know nothing, or almost nothing, about child prostitution and it is not very clear to me, from my height of 5 feet 2 inches, how I can be of any help to them. Tim insists, tries to convince me; a bit of a manipulator, he insinuates that my refusal could harm my future job applications. The discussion goes on for hours. He is firm. I am stubborn. I turn down Taiwan but I accept the mission in Thailand. Departure is scheduled for next month.

Terre des Hommes has obtained eighty visas from the Swiss government for refugee children younger than sixteen years old who have been living in difficult conditions for several years. My job is to put a name on each visa, issued blank. At the offices of the High Commission for Refugees in Geneva I meet Mary Pettevi, a slip of a woman with brown hair and large eyes that seem to take up most of her face. She is from Cyprus, attractive, very humane but firm in negotiations. If I owe the success of this future mission to someone, it's her! Mary conducts the meeting and draws an extremely precise picture of the obstacles we will encounter. Pol Pot's regime began ten years ago in Cambodia and, therefore, there is no hope of finding very young children, who would be the easiest to integrate into Swiss families. Only distressed adolescents are left, children who have been secluded behind barbed wire for the past five to seven years, children affected with serious illnesses and physical handicaps. Mary knows the joy of refugees who are accompanied to the airport but she also knows the obstacles, the difficult adaptations they face and the attitude of our society, which never gives anything away lightly. The choice of each child is, therefore, fundamental. Mary procures all the authorizations to enter the camps and assures us the full collaboration of her colleagues in Bangkok. I feel that I can trust her completely and I know I am not going to regret it. At Mont-sur-Lausanne many people are already taking credit for the project. Come on! So the world of associations is not very different from certain enterprises with their rivalry and their fights for power.

At the train station in Lausanne this Sunday in October it is cool on the platform. Families are waiting for the train to Zurich, children are stamping their feet and three grandmothers are sitting on a wooden bench eating cake. In the train compartment, I look in my bag for my travelling companion, an old, worn copy of *The Little Prince* by Saint-Exupry. My airline ticket is in my pocket. Departure time is 10:30 p.m., destination Thailand, non stop. Good luck!

Bangkok. Getting off the plane, I am once again immersed in the Asiatic confusion of this city's perpetual melting pot. At first, the taxi moves along at full speed, then the traffic gets thicker and the driver is obliged to slow down; cars are stuck bumper to bumper and we have to wait until the police come to untangle the traffic. To the left, women wrapped in rags are engulfed in the dust from a building under construction. They work fifteen hours a day carrying buckets of water or carting sacks of gravel, living on the job site surrounded by their children. On the right hand side of the road, beyond the tracks, shacks built in a haphazard way, with no water or electricity, shelter the homeless, those who have no job and no decent lodging. A little ten-year old girl is walking on the side of the road. She is wearing the compulsory uniform of Thai schools. Her white blouse is perfectly ironed. I can imagine her cardboard house and the difficulties her mother has to send her to school. The police finally arrive, the taxi moves again and we arrive at the Swan Hotel. The receptionist gives me the key to No. 406, and I drag my suitcase that weighs thirty-three pounds up to the fourth floor. The room is small but sunny. The monotonous noise of the fan gives the room a pleasant air. A shower and to work! I confirm my appointment at the offices of the High Commission for Refugees. In Brussels, a friend gave me a package full of food to deliver as soon as possible to Patrick Van De Velde, a Belgian on this side of the world. Patrick is responsible for UNBRO, the United Nations operation in charge of displaced persons on the border between Thailand and Cambodia.

Here I am, stuck in the 8:00 a.m. traffic jam. Thick smog, a mixture of exhaust fumes and industrial pollution, covers the city. The traffic moves at a snail's pace through the Chinese quarter. Patrick, the Belgian, describes to me the situation on the border and the moment's priorities. At the High Commission for Refugees offices he introduces me to the personnel, who will prove to be a precious help. Patrick will become a friend. At the end of the hall, Pierre Jambor, a dark, pleasant Italian, is speaking to representatives from organizations who have come to complain about the dramatic conditions of the refugees. He prefers those who propose concrete actions in an untrembling voice. A fax from Mary Pettevi, underlined with a heavy red line, lies on the desk. I explain our objectives and our questions: is the High Commission for Refugees offices in Bangkok ready to collaborate? If so, how?

Pierre Jambor smiles and calls his assistant. A small Asian with a lively look enters the room. Pierre advises us to get to work right away:

he wants a plan in three days. Efficiency. We work late into the night. The table is strewn with large sheets of paper covered with names and information: details of the whereabouts of each child, handicaps, particular traumas, date of entry into the camp, etc. From time to time a head bends over us: Patrick stops long enough to kid with us. In twenty-four hours of intensive work, we have checked one hundred and four little candidates. Now we have to meet the children. It is time to go to the camps. We have been driving for more than four hours and now we are approaching the Cambodian border. The countryside is pretty and the rice paddies are almost green. It is hard to imagine that less than twenty miles separate the Cambodian refugees from their roots. A wooden sign indicates the camp of Kao-I-Dang. Barbed wire encircles the perimeter of the camp and reminds me of Phanat-Nikom. Twelve thousand refugees have been living here for many years, waiting for a third country. In the distance, a lone tree stands on a dirt mound. My interpreter says: "Yesterday, another man, twenty-two years old, hanged himself from this tree. His dossier was rejected by an embassy. For the fifth time." The young man had arrived in Thailand in 1979 under the fire of Pol Pot's soldiers. And he thought he was saved. This is a common story here.

A child comes forward. Chem, twelve years old, registration number 67895, drags behind him an absolutely distraught old lady. His mother has survived advanced malnutrition but she remained handicapped in direct consequence to the shocks suffered under the Khmer Rouge regime. Chem is not an orphan: he will never be accepted by a third country.

Since I arrived in the camp, I notice that people are looking at me with expressions of hope on their faces. As usual, a stranger's arrival here is perceived by a refugee as a new chance, perhaps the last, to be heard by an embassy and to be considered as a candidate for departure, towards America preferably, that mythical country where everything is possible. This becomes more and more rare. Intellectuals and qualified men - "productive" people - have already been chosen by the hosting countries. At this moment, the population of Kao-I-Dang is mainly composed of illiterate farmers and people who have been rejected.

A small office is put at my disposal. Families congregate in front of my door. Mothers carry babies in their arms, some of them handicapped. I see a small mongoloid with a bloated head and a little girl a few years old with a twisted leg. A father caresses his child's head. The little girl's skin is blackened from a horrible burn, and little remains of her face that seems human. There are hundreds of people hoping; I feel ridiculous with my eighty visas for Switzerland. A few miles away, on the Cambodian borderline, the explosion of a mine resounds. Peace seems far away.

A child has timidly pushed his way through the door; he sits, greets me with joined hands. Sofan is eleven years old and missing one leg; he recites his story for the fifth or sixth time, observing my every reaction. The next child is a girl, born in the camp and abandoned four years later by a mother in distress. She holds a small bundle on her lap, as if she hopes to leave with me this evening. Five days later, I have succeeded in completing only twenty-seven files. No more. Clinging to my work table, I have listened to every child and tried to understand each situation; I visited their lodging: my presence spread hope. And I must abandon most of them and stamp on their file: "File without follow-up!" I think again about the stories I have been told, about the Khmer Rouge, about the reign of Pol Pot. Where were we all those years? The borders of Cambodia were closed and we looked the other way.

Another stop, another camp, another office: a child comes into the room, bows gracefully and places his file on the little table. Sounsri tells his story, stopping and starting as if it were a school exam. This twelve-year-old boy has been living in the camp almost seven years. He arrived at the border dragging a little three-year-old sister behind him. In December 1980 he walked through the forest with his mother and his sister, Koum. It was only four days to the border with Thailand. Walk, don't think, not of the traps or the mines. Finally, they arrive! The border is just three hundred yards away. Near them, a hissing scream rips through the night, a body, thrown in the air by the blow, falls to the wet ground. A man lies dying, his leg ripped off. Koum's mother turns away and closes the children's eyes against her. Sounsri remembers barriers at the boundary, men dressed in black and Thai soldiers. There are still a few more yards to go. A noise resounds, a hissing. And the mother drops the child. The woman's long dark hair is covered with blood. Beside her, the children have not understood. Other refugees are running like crazy, a man clutches the two children in his arms and drags them away. Since then, Sounsri is registered with the High Commission for Refugees, section "Unaccompanied Children."

Suddenly the boy stiffens on his chair and tears roll down his cheeks. The interpreter tries to console him but the little boy throws himself on the table, rips out the center page of his file and stamps his refugee paper underfoot. He shouts in Thai, and Koi, my interpreter, translates every word of what he says. I understand at last: Sounsri's sister disappeared from the camp after eleven days. He looked everywhere for her, but no one knows where this little eight-year-old girl has gone. Little by little the child calms down and a teacher takes him toward his lodging. This story nails me to my chair. Speechless, I turn my head toward Koi. His expression is that of a wounded man. The camp director had done nothing. He isn't here now, but it doesn't cost him anything to wait! I make an appointment to see him the first thing tomorrow morning. On our way back to the hotel there is a heavy silence in the car . Even so, my intuition tells me that this young twenty-year-old interpreter is going to change the course of my life.

Ten thirty p.m. It is cool. I preferred not to go out for dinner. Outside, night has fallen, the dining room was empty and from my window I can see the deserted street. Suddenly there is a knock on my door. Just the time to throw on a T-shirt and I find myself face to face with Koi the interpreter. He looks like a high-school student, dressed in jeans and a green jacket. With one finger over his lips, he makes a sign for me to follow him. There is a little gleam in his eyes. This walk in the night takes us toward the outskirts of town to the banks of the river. We walk quickly, without a word, bound by a mutual trust. Two young women are sitting on a bench, waiting in the shadows. Koi begins the conversation and translates the exchange of words into French for me. The two Thai are teachers in the camp where Sounsri's sister disappeared. The first one comes forward, she wants to speak. She whispers: "Refugee children disappear regularly. The soldiers take the little girls to supply the brothels of Bangkok. The little boys are sold as workers for clandestine factories. These networks also exist in the other camps along the Cambodian border. And we can't do anything about it! In Thailand, it's the Chinese Mafia that organizes the commerce of children." She stops, hesitates. "We are taking a big risk by telling you all this. Promise us that you won't mention our names in your report. Here are the names of two friends to contact in the camps of Kao-I-Dang and Phanat-Nikom. The situation is exactly the same there." Phanat-Nikom! The camp where I had been, the camp of Mr. Hoa, Mrs. Surin and the little cloth puppets. We leave them with a wave of our hand. The two thin silhouettes disappear into the night. I look around me again; it seems they never existed. It will be impossible for me to close my eyes tonight.

The next morning, the person in charge of the camp, a man of about fifty, is standing in his office, straight and sure of himself. But his words sound false: "It seems that the children run away and don't come back. We can't do anything..." He doesn't say anything more. Now that she has disappeared, Sounsri's sister is just a file number. Nothing more. Except for the person that bought her for fifteen or twenty thousand bahts.

Time is passing and I have to pursue my way. I still have thirty-four children to meet. Sounsri is left alone. I take my pen and write a note on the back of his file so that this child will have priority. Now I have to visit eleven children in Section 'C' at Phanat-Nikom. Six weeks have gone by since I arrived in Thailand. It is time to take a break in order to put a little distance between all these stories and my life. I spend a few days by the ocean.

I regret this mission a little; it gives me a false impression of rescue. At each meeting with a refugee, I ask myself why I have to save one to the detriment of another. There are two hundred fifty thousand and we will take out only eighty. Behind the term "identification" is hidden the word choice. Selection. Here, it is a question of choosing human beings.

We keep going. Phanat-Nikom hasn't changed, but many families have left the camp for foreign countries. Just like every Tuesday, the distribution of rice from the United Nations brings together the heads of families or houses. They stand in line, waiting in silence for bags of rice and dried fish. Mrs. Surin is still there. Her departure is scheduled for next month: "A little more patience!" she says. Our reunion, full of tenderness, takes place in the only restaurant in the camp, the same one where we got acquainted fifteen months ago. I tell her about my visits to the various camps and this mysterious disappearance of the children. With a bitter smile, Mrs. Surin confirms that as early as 1980 scores of children were disappearing along the border. Thai families buy their servants this way; others re-sell very young Cambodians to the brothels. That means that the network has existed for a long time and functions extremely well. I inform *Terre des Hommes* and wait for their go-ahead to start closer investigation. I want to know if such commerce exists. The network's mechanism must be discovered, its consumers found.

At Phanat-Nikom, on the other side of the road that I took dozens of times, I search section "C". Behind the two hundred yards of barbed wire, nine thousand Vietnamese wait desperately for a third country. One thousand five hundred of them are "unaccompanied" children. The survey/evaluation has reached its end. I have distributed hope. I hope that the humanitarian machine in Lausanne will work well. For the second time in two years I leave Phanat-Nikom, this camp I ran away from when nine of my pupils disappeared. I came back to wrest eighty of them from the world of barbed wire. Instead, this time, I discovered the horror of traffic in children.

I ask myself more and more if these disappearances aren't going to change the course of my life. Once again, Grandmother Simm, I think about you. You are the only one who can help me to find the answer.

5.

PATTAYA: ENCOUNTER WITH
THE CROCODILES

Back in Bangkok, I wait for Tim to pass through so we can review each file before mailing them. And to spend a night on the coast with him to try to flush out these child prostitutes who live in the bars along the beach. While waiting, I have identified a hotel in Bangkok in the famous quarter of Patpong, where children are placed at the disposal of the tourist clientele. I have also launched appeals to Thai associations in order to find a partner who can help me. Seriously speaking, I obviously haven't got a chance of entering this semi-clandestine environment. A blond woman with blue eyes! Tim seems satisfied with the refugee children's evaluation and he proposes to verify if the hotel in question furnishes children. A few hours are enough for him to meet two little boys. The next morning we leave for Pattaya, a beach resort located about seventy-five miles from the capital. Pattaya has gained an international reputation since the time of the Vietnam war when it became a mecca of prostitution. Guides in Bangkok, retained by hotels, bars, or simple tearooms, give ample information about the possibilities of Pattaya-the-whore. We have received information about the existence of a bar, the Boxing Siren, where children wait in the back room for customers before going to their hotel for a few hundred bahts. The driver of the rented car drops us on the main street. It is nine p.m.; we stroll down the sidewalk. Both sides of the street are lined with bars, Thai boxing halls, clinics for venereal diseases and brothels where hundreds of tourists from the West look over the merchandise displayed - like at the zoo. Girls of all ages, a frozen smile on their lips, wait for a customer who will pay a few dollars.

During dinner, Tim tries to explain to me what a man can feel in such an environment. I have a hard time following him. To me, this seems exactly like slavery, a gigantic human market where everything can be rented or bought. About eleven p.m. we separate, each one on a search for children. I pass from bar to bar. Unconsciously I still hope that we will not find anything. Fifty yards away I can see a neon sign and a name in color: Baby Bar. I take a seat on a high red plastic stool. Tired-eyed waitresses fill glasses with "Mékong", a bad local whiskey, while some German tourists comment in a loud voice about the figure of one of the girls. My nose buried in my lemonade, I feel terrible in the middle of this mob. The man on my left is German, short and fat with a face like a fish. Gently, he gives me a nudge to begin the conversation. Helmut is an habitué of Pattaya. He has been coming here regularly for seven years, three weeks in the summer, two weeks at Christmas. Here he spends everything he has earned in eleven months working in an insurance office in Munich. The only thing he lives for is to come back here, to the "country of smiles." To avoid wasting time, Helmut buys a bus ticket from Bangkok airport directly to Pattaya. There, he goes to a small hotel a few hundred yards from the main street. He lives at night, sleeps during the day and seems to know all the girls in the bar. For him everything is simple, the life of the prostitutes is easy and permits them to support an entire family. "The girls even learn foreign languages by contact with tourists," says Helmut in a throaty voice rolling his R's. Come on! Another few minutes and a couple of more beers and he undoubtedly will explain to me the therapeutic benefits of being a prostitute in Pattaya. Nevertheless, this year Helmut has come to find the ideal woman, the one he will take back to Germany after a quick marriage at his country's embassy. "Ah, the Thai! They don't need anything, don't ask for anything and are always smiling," says Helmut, going off into a long monologue about the qualities of these women. One thing appeals to him more than any other: submission. I leave.

A little farther on down the road, young children, five, six and seven years old, are selling candy and cigarettes. Thai law forbids children under sixteen to work. At the corner a policeman on duty looks the other way: blind or accomplice. A child goes up to him, his stock of merchandise on his shoulder. He might be six years old and measures barely three feet. As for the policeman, he has been transformed into a statue beneath the neon lights from the bar and doesn't seem to frighten anyone. Strange... this bar resembles a merry-go-round. Little vendors, knee-high to a grasshopper, play tag among the clients. Now it is already well into the night and a child of six or seven climbs onto my lap. He coils up against me and gulps down my glass of soda. This tiny kid is only looking for a little tenderness. Ten minutes later the child is jerked away by the person next to me. From lap to lap, customer to customer, the child reaches the other end of the counter. A man of some forty-odd years begins to caress him. His muscular arm encircles the child's frail body. With a repetitious movement, his hand moves on the boy's upper thighs. To judge from his self-assurance, this is not the first time he has done this. His face flushes under the effect of emotion or alcohol. He puts some red bills on the table, several hundred baht. The child looks at the money and the tourist. A heavily made-up waitress picks up the bills. The deal is made; the man is already standing up, he takes the child by the hand and leaves the bar. I am stunned, it takes me a while to understand. The man and the child are already far away.

Beside me a pudgy Italian attracts my attention. He is holding a little boy of seven or eight tightly against him. The look on my face must have betrayed my questions. Mario, thirty-three, begins the conversation. What is a young European woman doing in a bar like this? He is an almost nondescript businessman who visits Thailand regularly to meet his cotton fabric suppliers. The man is rather nice: Neapolitan, a good father, at the head of a clothing factory. He ends each trip with a week in Pattaya. The conversation changes and I question him about his meeting with this little boy to whom he seems so close. Mario smiles broadly:

- Prostitution here doesn't mean anything. Selling their bodies when they are children is part of the economic opportunities. Here it's the fathers who initiate their children.

I don't know very well how to react. Clearly he is not joking, he is not trying to provoke me, and he seems convinced of what he is saying. I cannot help but imagine us sitting on the terrace of a café in Rome, a chance meeting while travelling, a normal friendship that could have hatched. I push the conversation a little further:

- Mario, have you had relations of this kind with your own children?

- Certainly not, don't mix things up, the cultural model is not the same. Our children cannot comprehend this kind of love. They are not prepared for it, says Mario making a face, and you know, it's a pity.

This time I attack:

- In Europe these little fantasies would cost you ten years in prison, but here you can rape children with complete impunity. All you need is a little money and a poor cultural alibi.

Piqued, he hesitates before launching a discourse about the liberation of mores, new love, ancient Greece....

Silence! Curtain! I have heard too much. I, too, feel like ordering a glass of that "Mékong" muck, to forget the voices of Helmut and Mario. And if there are other bars like this one, with other Mario's, other Helmet's? I can't believe it. I get up.

On the street I notice another bar where children are playing. Mamaya Bar is similar to all the others with its illuminated counter, its high red plastic chairs, its deafening music and its girls who dance unenthusiastically. Some tourists are slouching on their stools; others, in better condition, are talking about their sexual performances and of their last fellatio in a hotel without any stars. A worn out waitress fills glasses of whisky-Coke. At the back of the room two adolescents, fourteen and fifteen, are fighting in a ring with a wooden floor. A boxing match where the punches rain and blood flows in front of the excited tourists. The betting is heavy.

We are about a dozen customers sitting at the bar. Two French men sit down, two young executives of some private enterprise. I can't help but eavesdrop. They are fascinated by their first visit to Pattaya by night, the hundreds of girls waiting for them, the girls' freshness and young age. They notice me. A few words, a smile and we joke about the grotesqueness of the situation. Philippe is an engineer. He is smiling, charming and direct:

- What are you doing in this place?

Good question. Quick! Make up something: I am a nurse in an infirmary in the quarter in charge of consultations for sexually transmissible diseases. I know enough about the subject; there is no risk that I will get caught in this little lie. The young engineer draws back:

- AIDS here? The tone of his voice has suddenly become aggressive. We are staying at the Royal Cliff Hotel and the Director assured us that AIDS does not exist in Pattaya.

I offer to send him some governmental statistics published in the *Bangkok Post* and *The Nation*, the country's newspapers. The figures are clear: four hundred thousand registered cases of HIV. Naturally the prostitutes are the most affected. Phillippe pulls his chair closer to mine, so close that I can smell his Ralph Lauren after-shave - and his fear. I find his adolescent eyes touching. Prostitution, contamination, AIDS, condoms.... The subject is launched and will take up the evening. His friend chooses to ignore us. He turns his back to us to protect his dream, but he has a peculiar expression on his face. These two certainly will not sleep very well tonight.

At two-thirty in the morning, in one last bar, I listen to a Chinese woman with a round face arguing with a man in his fifties. They are negotiating the price for a little fourteen-year-old girl prostitute. The conversation has become very loud:

- I'll give you six hundred francs!

- No. You asked for a virgin. You have her. If you want her, it's one thousand francs!

- Eight hundred francs. Last price!

She nods her head, the deal is made. In Thailand this woman is a "Mamasan," the name used for procurers. These women, often former prostitutes, organize the hiring or sale of girls. The teenager is waiting for her client in a room in the beauty parlor across the street from the bar. The man is from England and looks like a librarian who could be employed at Victoria Library. Stiffly the man gets up and crosses the street.

In the bar nothing has changed. I look at my watch ten times. At three-thirty the man is back; he goes to the bar and sits down to the right of the counter. His shirt is unbuttoned and his cheeks are flushed. The "librarian" is not the least worried about his appearance. One of his friends asks him a few questions. Both of them have had too much to drink. The "librarian" comments about the figure of the girl-child and the positions he made her use. His friend looks very excited. And I have to fight not to vomit. It is time to get out of here. I stop a moment in front of the beauty parlor; everything is dark. Walk! Put some distance between me and them. Between me and her.

The night is black and almost calm. The sound of waves can be heard in the distance. Drunken tourists try to find their way dragging tired girls behind them. I cross an alley, relic of old Pattaya from the fifties when this end of the beach was not yet an open-air cesspool. A

Thai man stops me and shows me a catalog. I cannot understand what he wants he talks so fast.

- Wait, wait. We have what you are looking for.

I stop, curious. The open catalog shows male candidates with little clothes on.

- Three hundred francs for the night Koon Madame; very high performing.

A quick glance at my watch indicates that I am already forty minutes late for my meeting with Tim. I run. In my mind I can see the faces of these men that fiddle with kids behind a bar, that look like "librarians" putting on a front of cheap dignity, the charm of Mario, good Neapolitan father that any mother would gladly leave her child with while she runs to the supermarket. What have they all got in common? I don't know. The kids, they must know because they have given them a name. I don't know if it's because of the way they catch their prey, because of their wrinkled skin or something nauseating that emanates from their clients, but the children will tell me one day what they call them: "crocodiles." Yes, that's right. The children are right. These men are crocodiles.

6.

BANGKOK: TOUCHING BOTTOM

It is four o'clock in the morning and I am still running. The lights of Pattaya go out like candles. I try to remember the way I came. In the distance I can make out Tim's silhouette sitting on the edge of the sidewalk in the light of a street lamp. The driver has dozed off at the wheel of the car. We leave this crazy city to go back to Bangkok. Two hours, driving in total silence. We haven't the least desire to speak, to share our horrors. I would like to go swimming to the point of physical exhaustion, to not feel the weight of my body and above all to not hear the buzzing that bores into my head. Daylight comes slowly as the car moves along at a good speed. On the highway the first trucks are already beginning to block the traffic. We pass several minibuses that are taking workmen toward the capital. How can they get fifteen people into one bus, packed in like sardines? We reach Bangkok as the city starts to wake up. The first joggers are already running in Lumpini Park and vendors are setting up on the sidewalks. Soup is boiling on transportable stoves waiting for the first workers to arrive. Tim has fallen asleep on the back seat.

We arrive at a friend's apartment in Sukhumvit quarter at No. 1 of a *soï,* those small alleys in Bangkok. The apartment belongs to John, a project director for an international association. I can still see his face, covered with freckles. A cultured man crazy about Chinese antiques, he speaks four languages but knows how to be silent. I never knew him to have a friend, man or woman. He has been away for many weeks now but calls me from time to time to give me some news and take his messages.

The apartment house is still asleep. Tim goes straight to the bedroom and falls soundly asleep; he is scheduled to leave for Bangladesh tomorrow. As for me, it is impossible to sleep, I am wide awake. Alone in the swimming pool I swim until I am exhausted; my arms ache but my head clears little by little. Since my earliest childhood swimming has always been an outlet for me. I leave all my frustrations, all my pent-up up violence, all my anger in the water of swimming pools.

One o'clock in the afternoon; the air conditioner cools the room. We come out of our psychological torpor. Mrs. Shen, the housekeeper, has prepared some Thai food and the smell of curry fills the apartment. She has that same dry thinness about her as those farmers who toil under the sun of the rice paddies. Sitting in the living room we go over each detail of our experiences of the night before. Tim followed a child, accompanied by a foreigner, to a hotel. The receptionist pretended not to see the child, who was shorter than the counter. Other customers came and the scene was repeated. The children were back on the street later in the night, a few bills in their pockets. I find it hard to tell exactly about last night. Something inside me fights to be forgotten, as if my mind refuses to accept these stories, as if we had invented everything. Tim understands:

- Talk, you have to talk so the violence you saw doesn't leave a mark, so this experience doesn't consume you!

I tell him. Mrs. Shen leaves quietly.

Tim prepares his suitcase. I already feel terribly alone. This mission involving refugee camps, disappearances and child prostitutes has changed something deep inside me. I must persevere, try to understand the mechanisms of this traffic in children, the reason for this omnipresence of Western consumers. However, I am afraid. Yes, I am afraid. I am twenty-five and I risk loosing faith in men for the rest of my life.

At breakfast Tim fiddles nervously with a piece of bread. I listen to his last recommendations. He authorizes me to continue the investigation for the two weeks I have left in Thailand. It is not enough. I have confused feelings about Tim. I have the impression that this idea of investigation/evaluation embarrasses him. I know that this is his field; he knows Asia and the children living on the streets of Bogota, Bangkok and Delhi very well. I would not want to create a sort of rivalry between us. I discard the idea. In the departure terminal of Bangkok airport Tim raises his hand one last time; a door opens and I lose sight of him in the crowd.

Alone in a taxi on my way back to the city I begin to reflect. I need direct contact with the child prostitutes in the hot quarter of Patpong. This is the only way I will be able to understand. The problem is that I am a blond woman with blue eyes; this is not exactly the description of a consumer. In Bangkok the children, or at least the little girls, are not seen. They are locked in hotels for tourists. Only the boys live on the sidewalk. I have information about "specialized" hotels that furnish clients with little girls under fourteen. Two of these hotels are on the main artery, Suriwongse Road. John helped me to find the guidebook "Spartacus", an eight hundred page travel manual for homosexuals. Thumbing through it we realized right away that consumers are most probably pedophiles. The guidebook explains how to easily find hotels where "young men" are available and how to procure them, but at eleven years old a boy is not a man yet. Spartacus uses this term to hide the network of pedophilia. Its eight hundred pages of filth are sold in all the capitals of Europe, in subway kiosks, specialized bookstores and sex shops. I have picked up tourist pamphlets in massage salons that indicated hotels where children seem to be at clients' disposal.

For eight days I have been passing my nights in the bars of Patpong. Foreign tourists frequent these bars in the early hours of the night before disappearing and leaving room for the regulars, often expatriates who settled in Bangkok a long time ago. Thai men leaning on the bar wait for who knows what. Certain bars close at two o'clock in the morning as stipulated by the country's law, but then the "party" continues behind closed doors. Girls dance on the silver bar to the latest American record, mechanical movements for bodies without enthusiasm. At night's end the customers' faces are bloated with alcohol and the prostitutes' eyes are blank from too many pills of amphetamine. I can't imagine how these very young women could live seven days a week in these conditions if they didn't take junk. I push open the door of Hotel S on Suriwongse Road and sit down among the clients in the hall, men from Western countries between thirty-five and forty-five staring at a television screen showing a Chinese porno. Two young Thai girls are kneading a man's shoulders, probably Indian. A European couple seems out of place. The woman is sad and pensive. The man, in his late fifties, has a round belly and thick hands rest on his knees. All at once the woman gets up and leaves the hall. A breath of hot air comes in as she opens the door. In the courtyard two children are playing ball by the light from the neon lighting; short red curtains conceal the cars parked in a row of garages bordering the inner court from where clients can enter unseen. It is not necessary to sign the register here or have a passport. Money is enough.

A man with his hands in his pockets goes to the reception desk; he has no baggage. A fat Chinese sitting on a high stool tells him the price for the room: two hundred francs for the night or one hundred twenty francs for two or three hours. Extras are separate and drinks are paid for at the bar. What is the difference between "extras" and "drinks?" Simple: drinks are limited to "Mékong-soda;" as for extras, that can only be girls. The client chooses the rate for a few hours and the Chinese takes a key from the board: "No. 121, first floor."

One thing is certain: I will need a partner to infiltrate the network. I don't stand a chance alone. The answers to my questions are hidden in one of these rooms. It won't be easy to find a man willing to play this game with me! I leave the hotel and walk the fifty yards of *soï* to the avenue. It is dusk now. Some adolescents cling together in a corner of the *soï*, their noses in a plastic bag, breathing an odor of burnt glue. My attention is drawn to someone sobbing. A European woman is sitting on the edge of the sidewalk smoking a cigarette with tears rolling down her face. She throws me a quick look, turns her back and goes toward the S Hotel. Her man is probably already there.

Since it is late I take a *touk-touk* back to the residence. The night watchman is sleeping soundly. In the apartment the light on the answering machine indicates four messages. John has called me from Hong Kong. He might know someone who can help me. I get a few hours' sleep before the sun rises. Since I left Brussels I have shortened my nights to five or six hours. I am bursting with energy and the phantoms of the past come to haunt me less and less. The telephone wakes me; it's John. He has an Australian friend, a man named Alf, who could help me. Alf has been in Thailand for four years, is manager of an import-export company and married to a Thai from whom he is getting divorced. I call him right away and make an appointment for late afternoon. Now I must hurry; I am already late for my meeting with the people in charge of the Foundation for Children, a Thai organization which, according to John, has some experience in questions of child prostitution. I have no idea yet that its leaders will play a major role in my project. The office of this association is located on the other side of the river. Impossible to find it. No sign of an association on this main street. I ask a policeman standing on the corner. It's hopeless, he doesn't understand. I rummage in my bag and find their telephone number; a secretary answers. O.K., I understand: a hundred yards from the phone booth, on the left; a garage door facing the street leads to the Foundation's office. I would never have found it!

The building is bursting with people, children and files; the atmosphere is very pleasant. The man who comes toward me will become a friend and an unfailing support: Teelapon, a young lawyer of thirty-five. He is big, six feet tall; he examines me with his small clever eyes and his smile is a real smile. He proposes a partner for me, a young Thai named Toy, who lives in the northeast. A little crazy but reliable. However, it will take time to contact him. In the meantime Teelapon the lawyer tells me of four hotels in the center of the tourist quarter where children are locked up. The S Hotel, which I saw recently, is on the list.

- Be careful, warns the lawyer. The hotels for tourists are the most dangerous. They are protected by the local Mafia and the police.

The Thai police, extremely corrupt and implicated in all traffic, seems linked to prostitution. We say goodbye with the certitude that we will see each other again soon.

Four o'clock: Alf, John's contact, is sitting on the sofa in the apartment. He is wearing a blue Chinese silk shirt that gives him an almost feminine air. I don't like his evasive eyes. Shen, the maid, puts a teapot and two blue porcelain cups on the table. The smell of jasmine has already filled the room. I explain my project to him. Alf reflects and says he will call me early the next day. I already know that he never will. I can see the fear on his face.

After three days of waiting, Toy, Attorney Teelapon's contact, will arrive this evening after travelling a good twelve hours to come from the north of Thailand. We have an appointment in a Vietnamese restaurant. I like this place with its artificial tree planted in the middle of the room. Strangely, one has the impression that this tree has been there forever.

I am early; none of the customers resemble Toy's description. The time passes.... Another false hope? Suddenly a man comes straight toward me: six feet tall, very big for the average Thai, dark skin, a white shirt worn with simple jeans. He sits down:

- You are Marie and I am Toy. Sorry, but my bus was late; eight hours on the road instead of the six it should have been.

We begin to talk. Just a few minutes are enough to have the impression that we have always known each other. He speaks slowly but he thinks quickly and accurately:

- O.K. I am going to help you. I don't know why; my intuition tells me I have to, that's all. So listen good. I am Thai and you are a foreigner. The rules of the game are different. You have a passport and an airline ticket. I don't have any of that.

- So?

- So I am the one who calls the plays.

Gulp! I swallow my saliva.

- O.K. Toy. Go ahead; I'm listening.

He calms down.

- I admire the foreign woman you are.

A shadow crosses his face.

- You have no idea what you are going to find behind those hotel doors. If we work together, it is only to observe. No rescuing. No child is going to be wrested from prostitution.

I consent; we finish our meal. The rules have been made. Toy's voice is more relaxed now.

We get acquainted. Toy works in a small town in the northeast, a region known for its long dry season and the poverty of its people. He is in charge of a social project in a shantytown and of support to unmarried mothers. He is married to a teacher and has a little daughter two years old. Toy collaborates regularly with the Foundation for Children.

- I can help you with your investigation beginning tomorrow, but I have only seven days. If the results are good, I can take off two months more next spring. Meet me tomorrow evening at the Petit Paris, a French restaurant on Patpong 1. At eleven p.m. O.K.? Goodbye.

And Toy disappears.

What an incredible meeting. For the first time in this strange city I am glad to walk alone in the night. In Silom and Patpong the sidewalks are crowded with clothes booths overflowing with copies of Lacoste shirts and Louis Vuitton pocketbooks. At the intersection for Silom, hoards of children wait for the night to pass sniffing glue and drinking alcohol to forget their misery. The same misery of all street children.

Foreign clients approach the children to talk price. They smoke a cigarette, offer some fruit and a little human warmth, and the trusting children follow them for a night in a bed, a meal and a few hundred bahts. You don't have to be a specialist to observe such scenes. All you have to do is stop for twenty minutes. And wait. Not far away a patrol of Tourist Police is watching out for the safety of these golden foreigners, the country's third source of revenue.

The next evening I am apparently early for our appointment. And terribly impatient. In front of the night clubs touters yell at passers-by soliciting customers: "Banana show at the Pink Panther. No charge, sir. Gratuit, monsieur!" Every ten yards a young Thai is barking the specialties of the house.

Toy arrives on time. Our program this evening is to visit the Suriwongse Hotel. We are going to take a room, pretend we are a couple and try to hire a child. We go over the scene ten times. We are finally ready to go. At the hotel's reception desk a fat Chinese sits posted on a high chair. We go to the bar where a porno video is playing on the TV. The Chinese hasn't budged. Toy approaches him, reserves a room for the night and pays cash. I get up and follow him without daring to look at anyone. I glance in the hall mirror to see if everything looks normal. Contrary to appearances I am trembling with fear. Room No. 224 second floor to the right of the stairs is a gray dirty room. The smell of mildew catches at our throats. It is an odor I am going to smell very often; I will shrink back every time. The floor boy is covered with gold jewelry. A knife hangs at his waist. Charming. For a time he waits for a tip then bluntly offers a little boy: ten, twelve or sixteen years old.... our choice. Toy makes a sign with his head and in a monotone indicates *"sip paï"* ten years old. I can hardly believe that things are so easy, the offer so direct, without any precautions - with a feeling of complete impunity!

All we have to do is wait patiently for our order to arrive.

Fifteen minutes pass before the door opens, pushed by a child's hand. The small ten-year-old kid goes into the bathroom, takes a quick shower and comes back to us wrapped in a towel. Toy talks to him gently in a warm voice and the boy smiles. He never takes his eyes off the toys we put on the table: a red fire truck, a bag of marbles and a small blond doll. Little by little the child becomes a child again. He sits on the floor playing with the truck. Toy sits beside him talking to him, trying to reconstruct his story. The boy comes from the north of Thailand, from a village in the heart of the mountains. The child's face lights up. He remembers the animals, the family cow, playing games on the dusty roads. Until the day a job agent passed. That was one year ago. Two women were offering contracts for factory work in Bangkok, one salary in advance and money sent every month, eight hundred bahts per child. Moo's contract, signed for one year, stated that he would sleep and eat in a clothes factory. The woman even promised to send him to school in the evenings. When he reached Bangkok, Moo waited two days in the agency's office. Thai men came and examined him very carefully; one man asked him to take off his clothes. Moo found himself standing naked in the middle of the room. The woman from the agency negotiated his price. All at once Moo was very afraid. He was taken roughly to a hotel and offered to clients. Every night, for more than a year, tourists have been sexually abusing him. His body shows signs of torture; his shoulder is covered with cigarette burns: the brothel keepers know how to get obedience and break all resistance!

A knock on the door makes the boy stiffen. Toy takes the tray of rice ordered, the door closes and the child relaxes again. He is afraid of the Chinese and the floor boy. For a long time Moo had hoped to escape; in vain. The children are never left alone. The little boy grimaces: he hates men, the clients. It is late; Moo falls asleep at the foot of the bed surrounded by the toys.

Toy takes a blanket and covers the body of this little man. I think: we have rented a very special hotel room, where a child is provided upon request, and we have offered a night of childhood to this little slave. And now? After a while Toy lies down on the bed staring at the ceiling, his left hand on my shoulder. It is too soon to speak and too late to sleep. Footsteps can be heard in the hallway: new clients. Another child is sent to the man in the room next to ours. To be raped.

Seven o'clock in the morning; Moo the child is awake. He dresses quickly, puts his toys in a plastic bag, opens the night table and hides the plastic bag behind the drawer:

- It isn't normal to have toys here, it is too risky for you, says the little kid who knows all the risks of this place. I will come and get them later.

Moo unexpectedly jumps into Toy's arms. Toy has just the time to catch him. He hugs Toy, waves his hand at me and disappears into the hallway.

I feel sick. My skin crawls with disgust as I stand under the shower with the soap in my hand. I stay in the bathroom for a long time.

Toy, worried that I have become ill, opens the bathroom door and finds himself face to face with me. He is embarrassed. We pick up our few belongings and leave. Toy is modest like all Thai everywhere in this country whether they live in the rice paddies, on the beach, or in the city. That is why, in the parallel world of night life, bars and brothels, this forgotten modesty is brutally transformed into cold vulgarity. Cold like this room, No. 224, that we have just left.

I will never forget that night nor the numbers painted on the door. In the Cafeteria on the ground floor about thirty "crocodiles" are enjoying their breakfast. They are between the ages of twenty-five and thirty-five, they are alone, they are eating. There is not one woman in the whole room. How many of these Occidentals returned a child this morning?

We share our table with a French architect, thirty-six years old, well-dressed, a good guy. He kind of clashes in this dirty gray hotel. I would have imagined him in a completely different setting, sitting on the terrace of a luxury hotel eating the finest foods in the company of a Thai associate. He looks nothing like the other men in this seedy-looking breakfast room. There must be an error. A taxi driver must have given him some bad information, or perhaps his secretary made a mistake in his reservations.

- Are you married? Alain asks us.

He seems curious about us being a mixed couple.

- Yes, six months. I met Toy through friends in London. We have come to live in Bangkok for a year or so.

Alain seems surprised.

- Is the Suriwongse the only hotel you could find? he asks.

Obviously he knows what this hotel is. So his presence here is not an error after all.

- The Suriwongse? It was recommended to us by a very good friend.

- Then you know about the facilities of this hotel? he asks in so many words.

I play dumb and ask naively:

- What do you want to talk about, its modest prices, its location in the center of town only twenty minutes from Patpong, or... its specialties?

- Its specialties, confirms Alain with a half smile.

The conversation progresses slowly. Between coffee and eggs the architect relaxes as if he thinks we came to this hotel for the children.

- I come here for work five or six times a year, he confides. I stop a few days at the Suriwongse to recharge my batteries, and then I go to the Oriental. I certainly cannot receive my clients in this hotel without any stars, you know.

We know. With a motion of his hand he calls the waitress and asks for more coffee. If I talk to him about Moo, the little boy prostitute, perhaps he will tell me about his nights; his key - No. 263 - is lying on the table. Briefly I tall him about Moo and the "excellent" night we had. It works. In a few minutes he is proudly telling us about his sexual experiences.

- Last night I met an eight-year-old boy that works here. He is a lovely boy with great sexual maturity. We spent a few hours together. I don't dare keep them all night, for fear they will steal something from my suitcase, you know.

We know.

- Very interesting. Do you speak Thai?

- A little. The basics. But the children are looking for a little love, not conversation!

Toy remains engrossed in his Thai newspaper. Every once in a while he throws an expressionless look at the foreigner. I know that he despises him profoundly. The French architect continues:

- Here the children become sexually mature very early, at eight or ten. Then they offer their bodies. They prostitute themselves because they have a commercial value. But they don't suffer! An adult can love a child physically without hurting him. The newspapers print any old thing. In Europe all sexual relations with a child are considered as abuse, as a horror. But there is something else, you know: new love.

We know. But more than anything else I would like to get up and leave, run away from you and your filth, you know?

Let's go on:

- Can you imagine this kind of a love relation with your own children in France?

- No, of course not. But it is a pity, because our relationship remains superficial. You are married to a Thai... a rare and interesting experience. When you have children, you will understand the father/child relationship of the Thai better. Can you imagine anything more reassuring for a little girl or boy than to discover sexuality with their father? Do you think it's normal that they should learn this from a stranger?

This man grew up in a well-to-to family, he studied in the best universities and he has children. I cannot understand.

The pedophiles I met years ago in consultation at the hospital momentarily come to my mind, because this kind of behavior is treated in my country. Those pedophiles had one thing in common with our crocodiles: their ideas, on the whole, have a logic all their own that no argument can penetrate. Alain has exactly this attitude, he won't listen to anything. The subject of conversation changes, turns to political changes in Southeast Asia, the opening up of Vietnam, the fierce competition between Bangkok and the city of Ho Chi Minh City, ex-Saigon, and night-life activities, which are picking up in the former capital of the communist South. Alain's eyes light up:

- I have just come back from a short trip to Saigon. Everything has changed there. The prostitutes have come out of hiding and loads of bars have opened up. I stayed in a hotel. Excellent! And they offered me children for five dollars a night. Of course I accepted. To get better acquainted with the culture of the country, you know.

We know. Five dollars, less than thirty francs, for a child. 'Culture' is very cheap in a country ruined by twenty-five years of war.

- I know the Philippines well, continues Alain. I have done business there, but the economic situation is a catastrophe and I don't enjoy stopping there any more. The people are poor, dirty... and the children are often sick. There, it is real prostitution.

I remember what Tim told me about the misery of the street children in Manila: their sores, their life on the asphalt, the beatings, the way they breathe glue, the look of age on their faces, nailed to a life on the sidewalk with cops on one side and crocodiles on the other. I really wish that Alain the architect would shut up!

Seeming to have sensed what I am thinking, he looks at his watch:

- Nine-thirty... already! I'm sorry but I have to leave you. An appointment on the other side of the city. I will be in Bangkok for another four days, come and have a drink one evening. Oriental Hotel, room 212. Call me, O.K.?

Toy folds his newspaper and drinks his coffee. The room is almost empty, a waitress is clearing the tables. I have no desire to see this man again much less have a drink with him on the terrace of a luxury hotel. But I know this is a mistake. If I want information about this traffic, I will have to accept to follow every track. But it is too hard. First of all because I expected to meet monsters. Instead, they all resemble the-man-next-door. This makes me sick. I need time to digest it all.

Outside, the traffic is dense, a cloud of pollution covers the sky of Bangkok, Toy is exhausted. We separate on the sidewalk. Next rendezvous this evening, eleven p.m., same place. I go back to my friend's apartment with immense pleasure, a real shower, sunny rooms and a reassuring environment. I force myself to take a few strokes in the pool.

Mrs. Shen, the housekeeper, came in on tiptoe. It must be noontime. I hear her moving around the kitchen, a smell of pepper soup fills the apartment. In a few weeks I will be twenty-seven. Behind me, the life of a happy little girl, a family without problems, a good student and the love life of women my age. Until now, I have been relatively spared. The first sign of destiny was the death of my father. But last night, without knowing exactly how, I passed through the mirror. I touched the bottom when I saw those child prisoners in the brothels. I will never be the same again. I am torn between the desire to continue this investigation to the very end and the wish to quit right now, to forget everything. But if I refuse to accept the reality of this traffic, I will never be able to look myself in the face again. In fact, I don't have any choice. I have pushed open the first door. Now I must go to the end of this horror.

The day has passed between writing this first report and a long, useless siesta. I always feel so exhausted. Psychologically tired. My head weighs.

I must get back to Toy. The traffic is thicker than usual. The first Friday of the month is the day the Thai spend their salary in the capital's big supermarkets.

The city is jammed, cars are lined up for miles. My *touk-touk* is stuck on Henri-Dunant Street behind an enormous truck that belches thick black fumes. Unable to breathe, my throat burning, I continue on foot. Patpong is at least twenty minutes away. Up ahead I spot the Jim Thompson Boutique, a shop with gorgeous silks, and stop to idle, looking for a little something for my grandmother. The bolts of silk hanging on the walls look like watercolors. Jim Thompson's is a long story, a story about an American who invested all his fortune to boost the commerce of silk, and then, in the sixties, disappeared mysteriously in the heart of Malaysia. The Thai love this story, which has become part of the country's heritage. Some think that Jim Thompson was devoured by a wildcat; others say he was an agent for the CIA.

Two parallel streets, Patpong 1 and 2, form the quarter with this name. It is said that it belongs to a single Thai family: the Patpong's. Many bars are run by Europeans. The most famous is on the corner of Patpong 1 and Suriwongse. It is specialized in banana shows, and for the past ten years has been run by a Frenchman who works for the famous Thai family in exchange for a comfortable salary and protection by the police, who tap a percentage of the intake every evening.

Another bar, slightly less popular, is run by a German. Later, I will learn from Toy that he left his country in disgrace, leaving behind him a failing company and large debts.

Toy is waiting for me on the cafe's terrace. He raises his head, pleasure showing in his little black eyes:

- I thought you wouldn't be coming this evening... and I wouldn't blame you.

We drink our coffee. People at nearby tables eye us. It is quite rare to see a Thai man accompanying a white woman. The opposite is common practice. A French couple in their sixties are watching the sights on the street with the greatest of interest: small-town tourists who are ending a typical tour offered by a large travel agency. They have spent ten days on the coast at Pattaya. Even though Pattaya Bay is the most polluted in Thailand because the sewage system discharges the city's domestic waste there every day, and even though American ships debark on its beach hundreds of Marines on leave, even if the tourism is wretched, this is an unavoidable stopover of every organized trip.

This evening we begin with a new tip. We found the name of this hotel in a tourist magazine. The R Hotel boasts its range of "sexual services". The article says to just contact the attendant. It even gives his name: "Roy".

The hotel is located on Suriwongse Road. From the looks of it, it is hard to believe that it hides a traffic in children. It looks like thousands of others: a large building, a little old-fashioned, its stars a little worn out. The attendant is sleeping on his chair: suit too big for his thin body, face with Chinese features, a strong smell of Mékong. Most of the keys are hanging on the board. Toy throws me an amused look and taps the sleeping attendant on the shoulder. The little man opens an eye, gets up, smiles at the sight of the magazine my friend is holding in his hand. Negotiations begin: two little boys for two hundred sixty francs. The price includes rental of the children and the room for two hours. Here there is only *short-time*, "courte période", explains the attendant. The receptionist hands us the key to 222. The large room doesn't look anything like the Suriwongse Hotel. The bed is covered with a flowered cloth, the bath towels are clean and a window overlooks the street. The attendant knocks three times on the door. The two boys enter and stand staring at their bare feet. The man pushes them into the room, like a master pushes his dogs. He insists that we give him half of the two hundred sixty francs now. The balance is to be paid at the desk. After use. He leaves. The children have not moved an inch. They are between ten and twelve years old, their clothes are dirty, and they have that sour odor of unwashed children. Quickly, they enter the bathroom. Back in the room, a towel around their skinny bodies, they lie down on the bed, eyes staring at the ceiling. Two little robots. Toy sits down on the bed, explains what will happen. This evening, no one will touch them; we just want to talk. The smallest one glances at his friend, jumps off the bed and takes the bag of glass marbles we left on the table. Sitting on the floor, he discovers this new game and the marbles roll around the room. The child smiles. He still has his baby teeth.

But Noy, the oldest, remains silent. Moving his body against Toy, he tries to seduce him. My friend keeps repeating that we are not going to touch him. The child continues his attempt of seduction. This boy has been acting like a child-whore for too long; he doesn't know how to act any other way. I will see a lot of these street kids, too aged, who have passed too many years in the brothels or dragging around the parks of Bangkok. By force of bargaining a caress to a stranger for a sandwich, by force of giving themselves to blond men thinking to find a friend, by force of letting themselves be trampled on, they have ended up believing that life is just this dull routine. Worse, they have lost their childhood forever. And when we find them, often all that is left is a provocative child with lascivious airs and an attitude of a professional prostitute who laughs when we talk to him about his misery, who becomes aggressive when we offer him a hand, who shuns us when we offer him anything else but money and a hotel by the hour. Attorney Teelapon will tell us that such children cannot be recuperated, or, at the least, are very difficult to re-integrate. Confronted with these lost kids, I have often wanted to drop everything. But more often my anger gives way to an acute feeling of urgency. We must hurry so that raped children will not become adolescents spoilt through and through. We must hurry before the streets will have done their dirty work. A race against time with all those "crocodiles".

In the room, the little boy continues to wiggle. Toy, annoyed, pushes him away one more time. The boy cries, disoriented. An hour passes. The younger one has fallen asleep on the floor. The older one, sitting on the bed drinking a Coke, tells us his story in a withdrawn voice. Noy is not a prisoner here. He lives on the street and works for the dubious hotels of the quarter. He gets twenty-five percent of the amount and is allowed to sleep a few hours in a room. He can't remember how long he has been living on the street. When we ask him, he answers, "Always." He doesn't remember having had a family and has been frequenting the hotels at least a year, ever since the evening when a tourist in Patpong proposed that he follow him to his room in exchange for fifty francs. The stranger asked him to take off his clothes, to lie on his stomach and to close his eyes. Noy remembers it all:

- He lay on top of me. I screamed, I was in pain, but no one came to help me. The man put his hand over my mouth to stifle my screams. When he was finished, I just lie there for a long time; I couldn't move, my stomach hurt too much. When I woke up, the man was gone and some bills were on the table.

Noy didn't want to do it anymore. But the attendant came looking for him many times on the street. The customers were waiting.

- I didn't have anything else to live by. I accepted. With the money from one client, I ate for two days. And had enough to help friends who hadn't found anything. When I don't work, we live in a gang of five or six; at night we sleep on the sidewalks or in supermarket doorways. In boxes.

As he continued to speak, Noy's bearing and speech became childish again. He grimaced as he thought about the tourists:

- They make us do disgusting things. I masturbate them, I do things with my mouth... and even worse. It hurts. They think we love it! I hate men.

He closes his eyes.

- When I grow up, I will have a wife and a beautiful home.

The other child is still sleeping, but his story wouldn't be very different from Noy's. Thousands of children live on the streets of Bangkok.

Two hours have passed, the attendant knocks on the door, other customers are waiting. The boys get up together, Noy throws us one last look, like an SOS, and disappears into the hallway. I am in a rage. I will never get used to this, never!

We pay the bill. The young Thai puts the red bills in a drawer and asks in a flat voice:

- Did you enjoy your evening? Come back soon.

Night has fallen outside. Toy suggests that we take a break before going on to the Suriwongse, but I prefer to continue to finish as quickly as possible.

Nothing has changed in the entrance to the Suriwongse Hotel: porno video, tired waiters, the fat Chinese sleeping on his high chair. The floor boy recognizes us, comes downstairs, takes a key from the board and hands it to Toy. Room 228: nothing has changed here either. A faucet is dripping in the bathroom, the sheets on the bed are gray, everything in this room arouses disgust. Leaning on the door, the floor boy proposes the various children available: four small girls from the north, no more than thirteen years old, a small Chinese girl, white, and a young Burmese, fourteen years old. Only Sonta is already reserved for a customer. Sonta! this little eight-year-old girl whom I have never been able to forget since we first met some months ago; Sonta, her eyes a deep well of pain. Every time we pass or come into the Suriwongse Hotel, I think of her. One of the golden rules for our safety is never to see a child prostitute again. Nevertheless, I cannot forget her face, that of a dying child whom I will end up buying to be able to get her out of her hell. But I don't know this yet. I only know that she is there, a few rooms away from us, in some man's hands. I clench my teeth.

We choose the little Chinese girl. The floor boy explains that she is no longer a virgin but she has had only three or four customers. She's new in the circuit. Therefore, the price is higher than for Sonta. A thousand francs a night, half for the first four hours.

Toy closes the door. Again that urge to vomit! Toy notices:

- Look, Mally - he always says Mally for Marie - you know we can stop. We can leave if you want. Right now.

The feeling passes.

- No, we'll stay for tonight. It's too late. If we leave now, it would draw attention.

I close myself in the bathroom trying to find a little courage. Is all this really necessary? I hear footsteps in the hall, the click of a door, the child has entered the room.

She is really a little Chinese girl. She has skin white as milk and, where her eyes should be, two little half-open slits above jet black pupils. Of course her face is sad. Never, in a brothel, will I see a child that does not have that same immense sadness. There must be something wrong with their eyesight when the crocodiles talk of sharing "love and pleasure."

It is impossible for the little girl to answer even Toy's most simple questions. She does not understand Thai but looks at us intensely. The girl is intelligent, she understands that we are not there to abuse her. With gestures, she portrays a dish of noodles: she's hungry. The managers of the brothels are not content just to make the children work all night; they beat them savagely at the least sign of protest and feed them barely enough to keep them from dying of hunger, just enough to keep them submissive, yet presentable to customers!

Toy calls the floor boy, who comes running:

- What's the matter? A problem?

Toy orders a meal for three and shuts the door in his face. A waitress soon leaves a tray in front of the door and knocks four times. Just seeing dishes full of fried noodles makes the child's face light up. She probably hasn't eaten much in the last few days. She devours two plates of large yellow noodles in just a few minutes. There is nothing we can do for this little girl whose language we do not understand. She points her finger to her chest, repeating: "Ly... Ly." Probably her name. She says something in Chinese and takes off her red nylon blouse.

She has a large sore on her right shoulder, a fresh wound, covered with dried blood. Ly grabs the notebook lying on top of my pocketbook and draws: a knife, a big man and hands covered with blood. The bastard who did this to her could well be the Chinese boss or the last customer. Here, any sadist having money can pay the luxury of a torture session with a child. Providing, of course, that he doesn't damage the "merchandise" too much. Or has a lot of cash.

I always carry a small first-aid kit in my bag. I hesitate: even the simple act of disinfecting the wound and dressing it could raise suspicion about us. But to leave her this way is to guarantee infection.

- Mally, it's a big risk, says Toy.

- I know.

- Here, the customers never take care of the children.

- I know.

Maybe this will be our last visit to this hotel. I am obsessed with the memory of Sonta. I want to see her again. Just once. But right now I have to treat the little Chinese girl's wound.

- Toy?...

_ O.K., Mally. We don't really have a choice. We can't leave this kid like that, can we?

The child undresses, the wound is already infected. I cover it with a disinfectant bandage and slip four band aids and some aspirin tablets into her pocket.

What a paradox! We are medicating a little girl prisoner. At her age, she is exposed to physical abuse, sexually transmissible diseases, AIDS, and has little hope of reaching adulthood. In these conditions, the chances of survival are practically nil.

Toy is sitting on the couch, his mind elsewhere, lost in his thoughts. He turns on the TV, raises the volume and speaks to me in a low voice.:

- You should stay, Mally. Ten days are too short. This investigation, this evaluation as you call it, will not carry any weight if we see only a few children. We have to go further, work one month, maybe two. And draw up a project for the children with the Foundation.

The blow strikes home.

- I know, Toy. But for *Terre des Hommes*, this is not possible. Another job has to be done: receiving refugees. I just hope I can get enough information. Then another person can take my place.

Toy shakes his head:

- I don't understand you, you people from the West. You go everywhere and then leave with papers for your files. You saw these children, no? You have to help them!

I strike back:

- Don't judge me, if you don't mind! The situation is already hard enough for me. Everything I've seen...this kid...her wounded body... her sullied look...

- Sullied by your people, Mally!

Silence.

This is the first time we have quarreled. I know he is right. But I also know that the Association will refuse any closer investigation. I am a woman. And the subject, controversial, disturbs. It raises too many questions about men's behavior! I know that I am going to make a lot of enemies.

The little girl has fallen asleep; stretched out on the bed, her body seems tiny, her face looks more calm. We have given her a night of childhood. For the moment we cannot do anything more.

It is four thirty a.m., the silence is total. Toy has dozed off on the couch, his disheveled black hair has fallen onto an old cushion, his long body is relaxed and his gold colored metal glasses have slipped to the floor. I lie down beside the child and sink into troubled sleep, too.

Seven o'clock, the noise of the shower wakes us. Ly has taken advantage of this opportunity to enjoy the pleasure of really washing herself clean. She puts on her clothes and motions us goodbye. The little girl pushes open the door and returns to her prison. She only speaks Chinese, but with a few signs and a drawing, she has made us understand the essential.

A tremendous feeling of distress overwhelms me. I don't know if it is worth it to continue. I feel spent, empty, ineffective. I cannot hold back my tears any longer.

Toy slips next to me and holds me in his arms in a rare fraternal gesture. He is Thai and does not have the habit of showing his feelings as Westerners do. He must have sensed how depressed I was to go against his modesty and reserve. We stay like this for a long time, unable to say a single word. The noise of a cart is heard outside the door; the cleaning woman has begun her rounds. It is time to leave.

There are only four days left before my departure, and we still have three addresses to visit. Their names were found in the all-too-famous guidebook, "Spartacus".

So far we have seen twelve children, written a report about each one and succeeded in taking some pictures. It is not much, but Tim, my superior at *Terre des Hommes*, refuses to prolong this investigation any longer. I don't have the time to go further.

Toy has arrived at the apartment. Sitting on the terrace in front of the pool, we take the time to speak about future possibilities of action. Only one partner seems possible to us: The Foundation for Children. We will go to see them again and try to draw up a preliminary project together before my departure. What I would like is for Toy to take charge of the follow-up to this first evaluation, become the driving force of the machine that will take the children out of the brothels.

Toy categorically refuses this proposal. I insist. Toy is furious:

- Our agreement was clear. I was to help you establish contact with the children. I am willing to wait until you come back, to be your guide a few weeks more. But to do a daily job is definitely out of the question! You are a foreigner in Asia, you have a passport and whatever money it takes to leave the country in two hours. I don't have any of that. I am Thai. In my country, a man can be killed for a hundred dollars. Less than six hundred francs... you understand? I agreed to help you in this action for personal reasons and I ask you not to try to find out what they are.

Toy gets up turning his back to me and goes to the kitchen. The discussion is closed. Even the screams of children playing in the pool cannot break the silence that has suddenly come between us.

We have spent ten days together and I know very little about his life except that a woman and small child are waiting for him in a town in the northeast. In his pocket he always carries a picture of a little four-year-old girl with a round face, slanting eyes and an enormous smile.

He works in a shantytown for some local organization that I don't even know the name of. When he leaves to go back, he won't even give me his address. Teelapon, the lawyer, will continue to be our only intermediary. So why this luxury of precaution? I can't even prove his existence. All I have is a first name... for a population of fifty-five million people. But I am an egoist! Deep down, I know he is right. He comes back to the terrace. Very professionally he says:

- We will meet this evening around midnight at a bar in Patpong. I would like you to meet a friend, an ex child prostitute who became an adult prostitute and is handicapped for life.

He relaxes:

- Will you meet me there? Don't be stubborn, Mally, you know that we always smile here!

He grimaces a smile and leaves the room.

It is already eleven p.m. The bars of Patpong are bursting with customers. At this time of the year it seems that the Italian tourists are the most numerous. There must be a hundred bars on the two streets of Patpong 1 and 2. I look for the neon sign of Gogo Cat's, which is located on the third floor of a building on this street. The sidewalks are cluttered with shops. I finally find the Gogo Cat's red and gold façade. I push open the door. A yellow light blinds me, the music is deafening, almost-nude girls are swaying to the latest Thai hit. Tourists are sitting around the bar in the center, their eyes fixed on the girls' movements; some of them are holding very young girls on their knees. Toy is sitting on a green bench at the back of the room. He is talking with a young Thai woman in a leopard-cloth costume. A young Frenchman near me is staring intently at one of the girls dancing on the counter. She is tall, her hair is pulled back tightly in a chignon, her underwear is transparent. Her sex is visible under the semblance of pants. The man makes a little motion with his hand and the girl leaves the counter. Another girl takes her place in the dance line. Toy comes toward me:

- There you are, finally! This is my friend Sowit, the one I told you about.

We leave this noisy, smoke-filled bar for a cafe two blocks away. The menu lists twelve different kinds of coffee. We order three expressos with cream. My mind wanders for a few seconds back to a small cafe on rue Montmartre in Paris.

After brief introductions, Sowit tells me her story, which goes back twenty-two years to a small village in the northeast of Thailand. Sowit is the youngest of six children. Her parents are simple farmers but everyone eats to their fill. One morning in May, 1978, Sowit cannot be found. Her oldest brother has sold her to a small Chinese factory for a few thousand bahts. Locked in the T-shirt factory, she works fourteen hours a day among the smells of glue and paint. The foreman, a Chinese about thirty, takes advantage of the boss's absence to lock himself in a junk closet with the little girl for hours. Sowit is raped and beaten for the least little thing. For fear of retaliation, she hides behind a wall of silence. Fifteen boys work in this room twenty by thirty feet where Sowit is the only girl. When a child leaves the workshop, no one knows what happens to him. Another boy immediately joins the group and takes his place in the production line.

Sowit is kept prisoner for three years. One night, the foreman's wife hears the child groaning from the room next to hers. She gets out of bed and sees her husband pushing the girl into the closet. The next morning, she pulls the girl into a corner and questions her. Sowit swears that the foreman has abused her many times. Two days later, while the foreman is away, the woman puts the child in her car. They drive for a good hour before stopping in front of a wooden house with Chinese lanterns on the balcony. A man comes out, examines the child and gives the woman a wad of red bills. Inside, young girls, nude, sit waiting on a wooden bench. At fifteen Sowit becomes the youngest prostitute in this brothel close to the Malaysian border.

A new nightmare begins. Locked in a room made of four wooden partitions, she suffers the assaults of dozens of Malays, who cross the wooden bridge at the border to come into Thailand. Malaysia forbids the commerce of sex in virtue of the Moslem religion.

Sowit, a captive, lives in semi-darkness. She loses the notion of day and night. Her only point of reference is the moment when a hand slips her a tin can with rice, some vegetables, sometimes a little meat. This same hand, a woman's hand with slender fingers, regularly brings her a basin of water.

One night, Sowit is tired. Seven customers have passed through the fifteen by fifteen foot shack. The last man gets up, buckles his belt and leaves. She wants to sleep. But a thread of light passes between the double doors. Sowit doesn't dare hope that... she gets up and carefully pushes the piece of wood. The managers have forgotten to put on the padlock! Outside, there isn't a sound. The neon is off and the bosses have fallen asleep. Only the watchdog moves its head. He knows her. Sowit hesitates a moment. A bark, an error, or failure could mean her death. But she can't stand this life anymore, the lines of customers, the boss's violence. She crosses the main room on tiptoe. The dog looks at her but doesn't move. A moment latter Sowit is out on the street. She runs. She runs and runs until she can't breathe anymore. A sign indicates a train station five hundred yards away. She sees a train in the distance; the noise of brakes and Sowit is on the train. There is not a sign of life in the compartment. She sits on a wooden bench, opens the window and breathes the fresh air of the night, the air of freedom. She is seventeen.

The train is coming into a station. From the window, Sowit can see the clock in the center of the Bangkok station; it is six o'clock in the morning. She is not familiar with the capital. Crowds of people are waiting on the platform to board the train, beggars are sleeping in the corners of the main waiting room. Sowit is hungry, but she doesn't have a cent in her pocket. She has worked every day for the past five years, but she has never seen the color of a bank note. She leaves the station, walks in the small *soï*. She is very hungry and her stomach hurts. She wanders for forty-eight hours. Free but condemned. At the end of her rope.

In her wanderings, Sowit meets a *mamasan*, an old Chinese prostitute who touts the merchandise for the brothels. The infernal cycle begins again. Sowit works at a bar in Patpong, dances on the counter and sniffs cocaine two or three times a night to have the strength to smile at the customers. She has thought of looking for her family in the northeast, but she knows it is too late. The return of a prostituted child, without a cent in her pocket, is a shame for the family.

During the rainy season one night in June 1986, she walks along a flooded street with a Japanese customer who has rented her for the night. The man is about thirty, wears classical clothes of good taste and a journalist's badge. Youri is a press correspondent for an important newspaper in Japan. He works regularly in Thailand and knows the country's language. In the room of a good hotel, he acts quickly, without passion but without violence. He asks Sowit to spend the night with him. It's late and the thought of going back to the brothel's dormitory to sleep in the same room with ten girls is not very pleasant: she accepts. After all, he paid her for the night.

Some days later Sowit overhears a conversation that upsets her. The manager of the bar is negotiating the virginity of a twelve-year-old Burmese girl locked up in a house in the Chinese quarter. She was kidnapped at the border. The British customer has written the address on a small piece of paper; Sowit has just enough time to memorize the number of the house and the *soï*. Sowit is twenty-two years old; the story of the Burmese girl is a little like her own ten years earlier.

She confides in the Japanese reporter, telling him every detail of the conversation she heard and asks him to help her. Youri, special envoy for a big newspaper, solemnly promises to help her. He says he will go to the house and verify the information right away. It is two a.m. when Youri leaves the room. All of a sudden, Sowit is overcome with panic. Why did she speak to this stranger whom she hardly knows?

Early in the morning Sowit goes back to the brothel in Patpong. Everything is calm. In the dormitory, the girls are sleeping on their mats. But two days later, the manager and his bodyguard drag Sowit into a car parked behind the building. They lock the doors and the manager has his 'bad day' look. Sowit is afraid. She thinks of Youri and everything she told him.

The car leaves the highway and turns into a one-way street toward a house. The car goes into a garage, the motor is turned off and two men roughly drag Sowit out.

Everything happens very quickly after that. The young woman is dragged into a dark room. Someone she doesn't know blindfolds her with a thick black cloth and other men are moving around her. She doesn't understand anything. An order from the manager forces her to place her two hands on a table. Deathly silence. Her hands are placed flat on the table about five inches apart. Sowit is afraid. Cold sweat runs down her back.

Unbearable pain comes from her right hand, a hot sticky liquid runs down her legs. Sowit's head turns. Her body topples from the chair and crashes to the floor.

When she regains consciousness many hours later, Sowit can see the overturned chair and a sea of blood. With her left hand she tries to feel where the pain is coming from that is paralyzing her lower right arm. There is nothing left of the extremity of the hand, nothing. Her four fingers have disappeared.

Sowit looks at me and modestly hides her mutilated hand under a big cotton shawl: "This is what happens to people who tell," she says.

The cafe is ready to close. Without a word, we walk toward the bar where our friend continues to work, this time as a waitress because the customers of prostitutes do not want handicapped girls. At the Gogo Cat nothing has changed, the girls are still dancing on the counter under the gaze of the tourists, the French man has left the bar with the girl of his choice. Sowit puts on her apron. Nearby, a big dark man is arguing with his friend, and bits of the conversation reach us: "Patpong is the showcase of Thai whores and child prostitution," says the big dark man. "They make big bucks, you know! And at least they don't work in the rice paddies up in the northeast."

They laugh. Sowit goes to their table, sets down two beers and takes the money with her left hand. She hides her right hand in the pocket of her apron.

Outside, the streets are almost deserted. In their bed of cardboard boxes or plastic garbage bags, rolled up bodies try to get a few hours sleep. In the distance, the show windows of Robinson's supermarket are still lit up, food signs blink in the night. This big shopping center is located at the intersection of Silom Road and Henri-Dunant Street, across from Lumpini park. Metal benches line the outside corner of the building. Pedophiles lying in wait for kids know the place well. In the evening, gangs of children run around the area begging or trying to filch from shoppers' carts. This evening, a crocodile is sitting on one of the benches. He is trying to seduce a kid of about ten by offering him a hamburger. The little boy approaches and throws himself on the package. He is dying of hunger. The man holds him by the arms and pulls him toward him. This game lasts until the child sits on his lap. I can see why the children call pedophiles crocodiles: they seize their prey like reptiles. We are standing on the corner of the intersection, less than twenty yards away from the man and child. The boy is lying on the sitting man's stomach. The man's eyes are closed and his hands press on the back of the kid's head. A repetitive movement shakes the little Thai's head.

Under Robinson's neon lights, a ten-year-old kid does fellatio for a pedophile tourist! Unbearable!

An instant later Toy is standing in front of the white tourist. The man gets up, tries to run. Too late. Toy lets go a punch. The crocodile falls back onto the bench, nose and mouth bleeding. He doesn't move, stunned just as much by surprise as by the blow.

Toy looks relieved. He laughs:

- I've been waiting for this moment for a long time, Mally!

7.

THE CHILDREN'S FOUNDATION

I put my granny nightgown under the pillow on my bed. The cotton material emits a sweet smell like only grandmothers have. Best of all, this evening there is a letter from Jean-Paul on my bed. The two-page letter written in his even handwriting is a real treat. We are so far apart geographically and yet so close. I fall asleep as day breaks.

Eleven o'clock: my head is throbbing from a migraine, Toy has disappeared and Chem, the housekeeper, has gone to the market. A note on the table reminds me that we have an appointment at the Children's Foundation. A message on the answering machine informs me that John will be back in four days. We will miss each other by just a few hours but I cannot delay my departure for Geneva. Too bad. I have just enough time for a dip in the pool and to finish my report. In less than forty-eight hours Toy will leave me to go back to his family in the northeastern part of the country. His train reservation is on the table in the living room. Did he forget it? No. He left it there on purpose to remind me one more time of his decision. This man is made of iron.

A *touk-touk* takes me into the Charoen Nakorn quarter where the Thai Foundation is located. This is my second visit to this association but I still cannot find my way. A half hour later, by force of error, my *touk-touk* finally sets me down in front of the garage. Païthoon, a man in his fifties, is waiting for me in front of the door. He is responsible for the Foundation's international relations. He receives visitors, administers donations and participates in all the international conferences. Païthoon has a master's degree in French from the University of Besançon in France, which means, of course, that he speaks impeccable French. He looks like a rather debonair professor. Païthoon did teach for many years and he could have easily finished his career in a school for rich people's children in Bangkok, but he preferred to come and fight in the ranks of the Foundation alongside Teelapon the lawyer. "Attorney Teelapon" and "Païthoon the Prof"!

The offices of the Foundation are located in the shadow of the building behind the garage. The rooms are decorated with pictures drawn by children and there is an air of peace about the place. While Toy speaks with Attorney Teelapon about our visit to the Suriwongse Hotel, Païthoon the Prof takes me to a room where four people are waiting. There is Sanphasit, forty, Director of the Center for the Protection of Children, a law student and an international specialist in children's rights. Next to him is Biphop, a handsome man about fifty with a good looking face framed by long straight black hair. The children call him "Papa Pop". He directs the village-school in Kanchanaburi deep in the bush on the edge of the river Kwaï. At Kanchanaburi, about a hundred children between the ages of six to eighteen, ex street kids, prostitutes, factory slaves and abused children, learn how to live again. The Center functions according to the methods of Summerhill and the famous British pedagogue, Neill, and the concepts of Buddhism. When a child is admitted to the village, most often in a state of shock, a teacher takes the responsibility of helping with the adjustment to this new life. They will face all difficulties together. Everything is allowed as long as the freedom of the others is not compromised. The village has its own school for these very fragile children. There are workshops for pottery and painting and above all a "children's council" that meets every fifteen days to hear what the children have to say. This is a unique project in Thailand, where pedagogy is still based on the teacher and his authority. It should be said that the Foundation itself was born under unusual circumstances.

In 1979, three years after the riots of October 6, 1976, part of the population took to the streets. A breath of democracy still blew in the universities of Bangkok. The students demonstrated for the abolition of the monarchy and rights for everyone. A big gamble! And the army did not appreciate it. Hundreds of students fell in front of the military tanks. The press closed its eyes and the authorities held the country in an iron fist. But the fracture remained. After that, one coup d'état followed another. Military leaders were replaced by other military leaders, but the structure remained the same and anti corruption programs did not halt the corruption. After the massacres, university professors, jurists and students refused to return to their desks. To fight openly was impossible, so they chose an alternative. They thought that in order to reform the future society of Thailand, they must begin to educate children in the respect of human rights, and they began with the poorest, the most miserable.

"Papa Pop" and his wife began working together with a handful of intellectuals; they opened a village-school and a nutrition center and gave social aid to families in shantytowns. Very soon, students and volunteers joined the movement. But it wasn't until 1984 and the arrival of two lawyers, Sanphasit, the specialist in children's rights, and Attorney Teelapon, that the Foundation developed a particular interest in enslaved children. The two men began investigating the network of traffic in children in Thailand. Backed with supporting evidence, they denounced the presence of little girls under age in the hotels and exposed the corruption of the local police. They were accused of being political activists; the Mafia threatened them. Nothing stops them. These are the men that are here in front of me today. They are ready to listen to me, to help me. Concrete help and solidarity.

Toy is impatient to begin. A Child Protection Center has existed since last year, but because of the lack of funds, its action is limited.

- With a reasonable budget, says Sanphasit, we could free at least a hundred children a year and form detection teams.

- It is urgent to open two centers, one for taking in the children and one to keep them six months, continues Attorney Teelapon. Preference should be given to their reintegration, their medical care and the beginning of a prevention program in the mountain region up north. The majority of the children we have helped come from that region.

Païthoon the Prof grunts:

- It's difficult to recruit personnel for such a risky project, no?

He grimaces:

- The Mafia is not going to welcome our project with a smile!

Outside, night falls as we discuss even the smallest details. Tapping on his calculator, "Papa Pop" estimates the probable cost of such a program. The line of zeros grows longer, the final figure is awesome. Everything is clear. All questions were pertinent. The team's professionalism is obvious from the way they work.

All I have to do is convince *Terre des Hommes* to finance this program. As we say in humanitarian jargon, the undertaking is ambitious and the local partner is dynamic and determined. All of this helps to reassure me a little and confirms my feeling that the idea must not be abandoned. I do not share my friend John's idea. He thinks that since we cannot take action and save the children, it would be better to reveal the contents of our report to the international press. Objective: publish everything and oblige the Thai authorities to act. I don't agree. This kind of action is premature. We cannot accuse a State if we do not have solutions to propose. Especially since the presence of foreign tourists involves the West's responsibility, too.

How will *Terre des Hommes* react? I promise to keep my new friends informed and to give them an answer within three months. We say goodbye confidently.

- I will not be the driving force of your action, Toy says to me smiling, but you have every chance with Teelapon. He is already dreaming of creating this project...

Toy suggests that we have dinner with Attorney Teelapon in the Vietnamese restaurant where we met ten days ago.

I love the decor of this restaurant: Vietnamese parasols standing in large stone pots, elegant bamboo furniture, the tree and its thousands of branches that fill the room. I don't know it yet, but this restaurant is going to become our regular meeting place for the next four years. Teelapon is really very captivating. Ten years ago he studied law to become a lawyer according to his father's wishes. He comes from a well-to-do family that owns an important business in the south of Thailand and his brothers and sisters are already working in the family enterprise. A brilliant person, Attorney Teelapon was preparing for an ambitious career. But he had a dream: human rights for his country, democracy, change. He would never become a business lawyer with a fancy office on the forty-second floor of a skyscraper: luxury and money do not interest him. He joined the Foundation and works for children's rights. His wife is a teacher, a tiny little woman that agrees with his political convictions and accepts the risks. In the beginning his parents remained obdurate in their incomprehension. Then, with time, they came to accept the fact that their son, Teelapon, was a fighter... for interests other than their own. Teelapon has been working ever since at the CPCR, Center for the Protection of Children's Rights. A dozen permanent workers and a good twenty volunteers and students work with him. The program includes requests for aid, reporting missing children, receiving children who are in a state of shock, victims of sexual abuse or maltreatment. The center buzzes day and night. The personnel localize brothels, search for families in villages in the north, comfort children who are waiting to leave for the village-school of Kanchanaburi, etc. "There's not enough time in the day," says Teelapon, smiling.

We talk at length and I have a wonderful evening, the first in many weeks. Only Toy has remained silent. I am dying to ask him about his past. But I don't, because that's the way he wants it. It's strange. Something divides these two men and yet brings them together. Attorney Teelapon is as transparent as spring water while Toy is mysterious. One thing is sure: our future program will need them both.

It is time to say good-night. Teelapon lives two hours by car from Bangkok and it is already midnight. He leaves us at the corner of Patpong 1 and Suriwongse. We walk toward Lumpini Park. I thought for a moment that the evening was going to end here, but Toy intends to visit a hotel he has discovered, located on *soï* Nana. A few minutes later we push open the door of a dubious-looking building. At first the scenario is the same as in all the other hotels we have seen. A young man around twenty or so offers us the specialties of the house. His photo album is incredible: women, small, medium or large, specialists or beginners; Asiatic men between fifteen and forty who exhibit their sex. A series of pencil sketches shows every position possible. Acrobatics. I hope there is a hospital open day and night to help clients in case of an accident!

And last, in a small notebook, pictures of children: a dozen small girls in ambiguous poses, "artistic photos" as the crocodiles say. The children's dark skin indicates that they come from the north of Thailand. Tonight, there are still three children to rent. The floor boy is in a hurry, but Toy drags out the game. Suddenly he looks the man straight in the eyes and says:

- You don't have very much for the price. Don't you have some animals that we could play with this evening?

The man stares wide-eyed. Toy lets it drop and says in a dry tone:

- We'll take room number eight.

Why this irony? I don't understand.

- It is not irony, Mally. If they could make money by giving monkeys or donkeys to customers, or by opening a children's brothel on the moon, they would do it. Believe me, anything has become possible in this damn city!

This is the first time I have heard my friend speak with such pain. He, too, is reaching his limit. We have been visiting hotels and seeing child prostitutes for ten nights now. It is time to end this succession of horrors. There is a knock on the door and the little girl ordered comes in.

I am sick of the same stories over and over! Why are we the only ones, out of fifty million inhabitants, who want to see things from the children's point of view? Isn't there any international organization ready to face such a situation? Don't Thai children exist in the eyes of international leaders? Are they excluded from the Convention on Children's Rights? How I would love to believe that I had invented all this, that none of these stories really happened! But the little girl who has fallen asleep on the bed here has those round brown spots on her body. I think of Alain, the French architect, and the words he used that morning at the Suriwongse Hotel. I can still hear his arguments about "affection", his "cultural" explanations, appalling pleas to justify the fondling, fellations and sodomizing of tens of thousands of kids. The rape of the innocent.

My mind wanders back to the winter of 1985 in Montreal...

8.

MONTREAL:
TREATING THE "CROCODILES"

The thermometer indicates zero degrees. I have come to the New Continent for a two-month stay. A scholarship offered by the French community in Belgium has given me the possibility to meet and work with specialists in sexual abuse and maltreatment of children. About ten miles from Montreal, there is a prison-hospital run by the Ministries of Health and Justice. The Pinel Department houses and is responsible for pedophiles and rapists condemned to heavy sentences, men who have abused, sodomized or sometimes even killed young children.

Dr. Aubut's assistant very kindly met with me and explained in detail their methods of working with these sexual perverts. Objective: cure them to avoid any subsequent offense. The medical team considers pedophilia a serious illness. Treatment is possible even if, as in some cases of recidivism, psychiatry has reached its limits. I insisted on being able to come to Quebec to participate in group therapy sessions where pedophiles, child victims and parents come together to talk about their problems. I was very upset by what the children said, the after-effects and the anguish they bear even after many years. Some were raped at the age of four, five, six or seven by someone close to them or by a stranger, on their way home from school or after baby-sitting. Tired mothers told about their daily burdens, the loss of an incestuous husband, the feeling of guilt for having understood too late, or having remained silent.

I remember having hesitated for a long time before attending a meeting for eight pedophiles in treatment, but they had no problem in accepting the idea of my presence. I went to the meeting with death in my heart, my mind brimming with the stories of children with whom I had spent a long afternoon. The group met in a comfortable setting several times a week to talk about this "obsession for children," which some of them still feel even after many years in prison. Outwardly, they are like men everywhere between the ages of twenty and sixty. Some of them were even quite nice and I felt sorry to think about them as child rapists.

In Europe, these same pedophiles are sent to prison for many years but are generally released "for good conduct." Never having really received adequate attention, they usually relapse. Almost always.

I am thinking about all this now in the hotel room in Bangkok with Toy who is sleeping and the little girl rolled up in a ball under the sheet. This is my last night here. It is time for assessment.

In Belgium, during my studies, I had my first contact with child abuse in the examining room of the pediatric ward where I treated raped children and saw first-hand the curse of pedophilia. I put it all behind me to live differently, I left to forget... but destiny decided otherwise. The last few weeks have been difficult. I am physically and mentally exhausted, but I have met extraordinary people, shared Toy's trust and gone beyond my own limits. The phantoms of my father, Philippe, and Marianne have disappeared leaving memories. Now Toy and I must separate.

It is almost three o'clock and Kualong-Pong station is crawling with people. On platform 1, families loaded down with baggage are waiting for the north-east bound train; on the other side of the same platform, a group of French tourists wearing colored T-shirts and carrying straw hats and umbrellas is getting off the train arriving from Chiang-Mai. The hat and umbrella people seem tired from the long trip. I see Toy in front of the cafeteria. Like all travelers, he buys provisions for a trip that will last longer than eight hours. He is by far the most elegant Thai in the station with his impeccable Levi's jeans, his well-cut shirt and his gold colored metal glasses that give him an intellectual air. We are going to leave each other. I cannot help but ask him again and again - what weakness! - to think about my proposal and take charge of the project himself. He looks at me and shakes his head:

- No, no and no. But if you come back to Thailand, I will be here to help you with your investigation. For a month, two if you want. But then I will disappear from your life. And you, you will continue to fight for these children. Don't ask me for more than that.

After that everything goes very quickly. Toy kisses me goodbye on the cheek as a brother would. And he disappears into the crowd of travelers. I stay on the platform for a long time, unable to move, a strange ache in my chest.

Toy... I barely know him. He spoke so little about himself, his life, his feelings that I know nothing, or almost, about him. I can still hear his laughter. Our paths touched without really crossing. But he came into my life. I am going to miss him.

9.

BANGKOK: WARNINGS
FROM THE CHINESE MAFIA

Thousands of watermelons block the road: the truck's trailer has turned over. The accident has blocked traffic for more than two miles, taxi drivers sit patiently reading their newspapers, not the least bit angry. I pay my *touk-touk* and continue on foot. Back at the residence, I try to call *Terre des Hommes* in Lausanne, but the construction sites near our building disturb the telephone lines. The phone doesn't work.

I head for the Hilton Hotel, a ten minute walk away; their telephone line is excellent and the people at the reception desk are very nice. In Lausanne it is exactly six p.m., closing time; no one answers.

Alone in the apartment, I prepare my baggage while munching on a bar of chocolate. Outside, lamplight illuminates the garden and pool; at the end of the garden, a walkway gives access to the street. A uniformed watchman, a young Thai about twenty, stands guard at the yellow and red barrier. During the day he goes to the university, at night he works to pay for his studies. He is always smiling. We chat together very often sitting on the bench beside the barrier. As I tell him goodbye for the last time, I linger for awhile and slip him two hundred bahts.

Across the street, workmen work day and night on the construction of a fifty floor skyscraper. The headlights of the trucks are on all night to illuminate these land rats that climb to the top without any safety harness; sometimes a worker, bone tired, loses his footing or misses a rung of the bamboo ladder. Boys less than ten years old hand tools and carry buckets. I recall the public notice by the Minister of Education announcing schooling for everyone! A woman, her head covered with a piece of cloth to protect her from the dust, waves to me. Behind her, a three-year-old child drags its feet. The other side of the coin of the famous growth of Thailand. From the twentieth floor of this luxurious building of the future one will be able to see the dining rooms and the turquoise swimming pool of the Hilton Hotel. I must get going! I cannot dilly-dally any longer, I have a flight to catch. Time for a shower to the music of Mozart, then off to the airport. I start to hurry. Everything is very calm out in the *soï*.

Suddenly something hits me violently. My head bangs on the door as I fall to the floor. Punches rain down on me. For a fraction of a second I can see the faces of two men. They continue to beat me. I try to protect my head. I feel pain everywhere. Warm blood runs from my nose to my mouth. There is a terrible feeling of burning on my forehead then on my shoulder and around my breast. I can hear someone run screaming toward my aggressors. The men are taken by surprise and shout something as they escape.

I'm dizzy, my head is turning, I feel like vomiting, there's blood on my blouse, all the buttons have been torn off. The watchman helps me to sit up. My passport and money are scattered all over the floor. The gold chain my father gave me is broken. But what happened? My body is a mass of pain. All at once there is a crowd of people around me from the other apartments; men and women crowd around, light a lamp, a girl in a blue smock holds a small bottle of mint under my nose.

My head hurts terribly. I have a bump as big as an egg on the top of my head. Numbly I hear a man say that he understood what the aggressors shouted as they ran away. Three words: "As an example..." With firmness, he takes me to the police station. The waiting room is full of people, victims of rape, accidents, aggression; in short, the environment of a police station. I have to wait a full three hours. The police officer declares that the motive for the aggression was theft, and he goes about writing his report in four copies, typing with one finger on an ancient typewriter. "Aggression for theft?" But they didn't steal anything from me! Neither money nor passport nor jewelry. It is obvious that they attacked and beat me as an example, to stop me from going any further with my investigations. Infuriated by the police officer, I leave the station without even signing the report. It is more important for me to get to the emergency room at the hospital.

There, a nurse hurries toward me, undoubtedly because of my white skin. Maybe also because of the sight of me, which I see reflected in the glass door... dried blood on my blouse, a wound on my forehead and a face swollen double. I look as if I've had a car accident. A doctor comes into the examining room. He is an American, six feet tall with blue eyes and a reassuring voice. He asks me to lie down on the table and carefully examines every black and blue mark telling me that my burns are deep and already infected.

- Cigarette burns. You will probably have scars on your forehead. The shoulder is not as bad.

The doctor writes down the time.

- Let me ask you some questions. If you want, it can wait; you are not obliged to answer.

It is two thirty in the morning, I am empty; a very gentle nurse cleans my burns, the touch of the cotton on the wounds makes me shiver. I agree to answer the doctor's questions:

- My name is Andrew. Tell me who the bastard is that did this to you. And why?

- Who? Why? I don't know. I can't answer your question. I only remember two men running away...

I tell him what happened and begin to cry. A flood of tears. I cannot get hold of myself. The Thai nurse leaves the room quietly. I am alone with the doctor, unable to say a word. He holds me in his big arms and waits for a long time untill I stop shaking from the sobs. I can't imagine what a Thai doctor would think if he came in. But I don't give a damn about appearances! The nurse comes back with a little paper box of pills and a healing cream for the burns. Andrew insists that I stay in the hospital forty-eight hours to be sure there is no further trauma. I saw the x-rays and everything seemed normal to me. I prefer to go home and sleep until the time of my departure. He offers to come to John's apartment for one last check-up before I leave Bengkok. I accept. As he accompanies me to the exit to get a taxi, he realizes that my blouse is not very presentable and goes to get me a clean T-shirt. I find myself in a taxi driving in the night through Bangkok. In the courtyard of the apartment building, the watchman is sound asleep. Thieves like my aggressors could enter and they wouldn't even be bothered. Good heavens! Here I am gripped with a fear I have never known.

Chem, the maid, has heard about the incident. She moves around the apartment. A hot bath is prepared. She pours in the contents of a green bottle and some herbs. She sets a teapot of camomile tea beside the bathtub. I slip into the hot water. Stretched out on the bed later, I let Chem massage my shoulders very gently. Little by little the pain gives way to sleep. Chem quietly leaves the room but I am immediately overcome by anxiety: I don't want to be left alone in the dark. Instinctively she understands and leaves the door half open.

Still today, I cannot close my eyes in total darkness if I am alone. This fear of the dark will never leave me.

The next day, I am awakened by the smell of coffee that titilates my nostrils. I begin by examining the extent of the damage in front of the big mirror in the bathroom. I can count the black and blue marks on the fingers of my two hands. My face is swollen, there is a 3/4 inch cut on the inside of my bottom lip, three cigarette burns mark my forehead and three larger ones mark my left shoulder. These small round marks remind me of other identical marks: those I have seen thousands of times on the bodies of child prostitutes.

Andrew, the medic, arrives and prepares breakfast under the watchful eyes of Madame Chem. The table is loaded with fruit, cereal, eggs, and thirty-six things that I absolutely cannot swallow. I suck on a piece of fruit that Chem wisely cut into small pieces. Andrew teases me; my first smile of the day.

Andrew is a homosexual and lives with an Australian. He doesn't seem to be a night owl, unless it's the kind working in the emergency room. He has been working in Thailand for five years and is planning to go back to his country in about three months and return to school to specialize in pediatrics.

Over coffee, I tell him briefly about my experience, the street children and the plight of the children who are prisoners in the brothels. He jumps up:

- Are you crazy? You could have ended up in the Chao Praya River. They wouldn't have written ten lines about it in the local newspaper. Unrecognizable bodies arrive at the hospital morgue every month. The Mafia is not very generous with people who decide to block their way. Act? Forget it!

After three hours of arguing, I forget the sting of my burns. It's late. We have to say goodbye, with a smile. This doc is a good doc!

I pick up the telephone and ask the operator for a number in Kenya; I want to speak with Jean-Paul. Two hours later I hear the singsong voice of the operator:

- I'm sorry, there is no answer at the number you asked for.

Nine thousand miles separate us. I am alone in Bangkok. Better that way. What's the use of scaring him? I check my bags and pass immigration control without any problems. Once on the Swissair plane, I fall right to sleep. When I wake up twelve hours later, the plane is preparing to land in Zurich. From the oval window, this little country seems to be caught in the ice of winter.

10.

NAIROBI:
THE FLAME TREES OF KENYA

At the airport in Zurich I can see the Program Director of *Terre des Hommes* standing on the other side of the big windows beyond customs. Why did he come all the way to Zurich to meet me at the airport? This is something very unusual. The fact is, a serious conflict has erupted at the office in Lausanne. Motive: the action in favor of refugees.

Part of the Board of Directors at *Terre des Hommes* wants to discontinue this mission. Some of them think that the children chosen are too old, too difficult to reintegrate. This is an interesting observation, but it comes too late; they should have thought about this sooner. Ten years have already passed since the genocide in Cambodia! The Board is going to meet in two days to decide whether or not to continue the action. Like a sort of right to live or die over the camp children. This is unacceptable! Edmond Kaiser also is furious. Edmond is the most complex man I have ever met. Some say that if he had not been the founder of *Terre des Hommes*, he would have been a great dictator. At the age of seventy, he is unbearable. But I will always love him and be grateful to him for the way he reacted. Because nothing stops him. A few phone calls, insulting letters, and he gets what he wants. So we won: the Board confirmed the action. Well! It was about time! The young refugees are going to tread on Swiss soil.

For the rest, everything is blocked. Tim is not here and I miss his support. With him away, the doors close one after the other. Then, one morning in December, a definite no is handed down; *Terre des Hommes* will not rescue the children of Bangkok. The aggression I was victim to seems to play against the project. True, the lack of security is a major argument. Upon his return, Tim proposes new contracts to me. But I

78

have no desire to go to Egypt or Lebanon. All I can think of are the faces of Thai children and their appalling stories. I am not one of those heroes of humanity who devour children from the refugee camps for appetizers, those from the brothels of Bangkok as the main course and handicapped children from Cairo or child victims of the war in Lebanon between a pear and cheese. I do not have the bulimia for drama.

I jump on a train for Paris. It's a four hour trip, four hours of anger boiling inside me. As soon as I check my bags at the luggage deposit, I buy a bathing suit and go straight to a swimming pool. I swim and swim. Later on, sitting on the terrace of a café drinking real hot chocolate, I look at the life of Paris. A lost American tourist holding a guidebook in his hand questions passers-by. A young girl in sexy clothes rushes to help him and leads him toward the wharf. How beautiful they are!

Down the street, adolescents daydream in front of a travel agency. A list of exotic destinations is displayed in gold letters on a black board: "Nairobi, 8,000 French Francs, seats available next week." Nairobi? Jean-Paul! I push through the door. In less than five minutes I have bought a ticket.

Jean-Paul is waiting for me at Nairobi airport. He hasn't changed. Hurrah for Africa!

I am already acquainted with Mali, Burkina Faso, and Senegal. During my studies, I did training periods in leprosy and nutrition centers. I love this continent, its culture, its festive air. You can dance all night, drink the local beer, live without worrying about appearances. Jean-Paul has an apartment twenty minutes from the center of town in a modern building with a garden and pool. Nairobi, the capital, is breezy and green. Some concrete buildings mark the presence of large international organizations, but life is still pleasant.

We spend three weeks visiting this country where animal reserves give the idea of paradise. As we track lions moving stealthily through the high grass, discover lakes, come upon thousands of flame trees, watch hippopotamuses as they roll in the mud, carefully sneak up on a group of elephants standing in a grove, observe monkeys as they hide in the bougainvillea, those tall bushes that resemble immense bouquets of pink flowers, I feel like I can breathe. In certain parks, cabins deep in the forest give us the chance to live in contact with animals that are still wild. Strange noises can be heard at daybreak: the last cries of a gazelle caught in the fangs of a lion, the rustle of rodents as they come up on the terrace looking for scraps left by the tourists. When a man dies, the sound of drums can be heard announcing his death. In the mourning village, everyone sings and dances so his spirit can enter the beyond. Traditional Africa! We meet an American widow who came to Africa in 1960. She runs a lodge for tourists and nature-lovers. In a corner of the living room hangs a picture of an old lion beside its masters. The animal died of old age, but the lady of the house still talks about him with emotion: "He was a real friend." In the morning, from this room, you can see giraffes eating the leaves from the trees. A dream.

Yet regardless of the charm of this country and Jean-Paul's love, not a day passes without my thoughts going to the children in Thailand. I know what is going on down there and I can't do anything about it!

Some nights, in the semi-darkness of the room, I see Sonta, Sowit, Sounsri and all the others. I know that I have to go back. Jean-Paul is upset. He wants me to stay with him and tells me about various projects being carried on by local associations that are working in the shantytowns or with street children. Of course I am enthusiastic about these projects! But I have to try to do something in Bangkok first. The weeks pass but the obsession of Bangkok never leaves me. Why? Why do I always see the refugee camps in Thailand, with their barbed wire, their guard stations and the orphan kids, semi-refugees or semi-prisoners? Why can't I stand the idea of them being kidnapped? Locked up, sequestered, raped? Why does this tragedy cause pain in my stomach? Very painful, incredibly strong! As if this is a unique drama. I have seen children die of hunger in Sahelien Africa, children affected with leprosy, physically handicapped children in Roumania, and every other kind of misery in all parts of the world. But I don't have the vocation to carry all the sins of the world on my shoulders. I can live, laugh, love. And forget. Everything except those children that go from border camps to other camps, those formed by the walls of the brothels in Bangkok. Why? I search for the answer, Grandmother Simm, and I recall the stories you used to tell with reserve and modesty to the little girl that I was. Stories of Europe at war, a Europe which had become barbaric once again, where men came and took children from their homes, threw them in trains and sent them behind barbed wire to camps from which they never returned. Isn't that the way it went, huh, Grandmother?

I have decided to tell Jean-Paul this evening that I am leaving Kenya. I am going back to Thailand for a month, just the time to finish my investigation with my friend Toy. We are having dinner at the African Heritage, a complex that is like both a cafeteria and a luxurious handicraft shop. Sand and terra-cotta colors, baskets from lake Turkana, chess boards in soapstone, handmade silver necklaces by artisans from the North: everything is a delight for the eyes. We have reserved a table in an Ethiopian restaurant. Sitting on the floor on embroidered cushions around a large pewter tray set in the middle of a cloth, we eat pieces of meat in a spicy sauce. We mix different kinds of grain into balls with our hands. We are a little awkward and the pretty tall waitresses dressed in traditional robes watch us with a smile. I have just begun to speak when Jean-Paul interrupts me: he understands the way I feel, and if I want, he will help me finance my program. Now we are bound by a new feeling, one based on respect for each other's liberty.

It won't be easy, I know. There are risks, and I have become a target. But if I can collect more information, I can make up a dossier to submit to other European associations and find financing for the project.

At Nairobi airport, my bags checked in, I have about twenty minutes before boarding time for Brussels. We look at each other in silence. I detest airports, train stations and all those places where hundreds of separations take place every day. Jean-Paul disappears into the crowd. But I am not alone anymore. I know that wherever I may be, he will be there at my side. And in times of uncertainty, I will have his arm to lean on.

11.

BANGKOK: SONTA MUST BE SAVED!

The city of Bangkok is the same as always, smothered in a cloud of pollution. Attorney Teelapon and Païthoon the Prof have been able to contact Toy up in the north of Thailand.

There he is at the arrivals gate! I can see him searching the crowd of passengers from three planes that arrived one after the other. Tourists are waiting in line at the immigration services counter. A quick calculation: no less than fifteen officers are verifying passports, about twenty passengers each time... three hundred people, mostly unaccompanied men. The observation is stunning. Thailand seems to have exchanged its luxury tourists of the '70s for people with ambiguous motivations, probably sexual. Noticeably, fewer people go to the Buddhist temples than to the hot sections of town. Toy comes forward. In the middle of this big hall where thousands have passed we greet each other with emotion and reserve. No demonstration of feelings in the country of smiles!

We go to the home of some friends of Toy's, far out of the center of town. They are a typical Thai couple with three children and an old grandmother. The three-story house overlooks a canal, a souvenir from the time when people living in the city moved about on the *klongs*, the canals of Bangkok. They do not speak a word of a foreign language. Toy knows the woman well, they studied in the same university. We are very safe here. After discussions, we decide to go back to the Suiwongse Hotel to try and find the children we have already seen in order to complete our files and see if we can find their families. My unspoken hope is to find Sonta. I cannot forget her face.

At the Suiwongse, nothing has changed: the Chinese at the entrance, the television screen, the porno film, the tourists at the bar and the same floor boy still sitting on the steps of the staircase watching out for customers.

Sonta is already rented out to room 220 for tonight. The customer paid for the whole night. We reserve her for the following night. For now, the floor boy offers us two little Chinese girls and an eleven-year-old boy: all the other children are already working. How many of them are locked in the garage-room on the ground floor? We try to question the floor boy, but he carefully avoids answering.

Twenty-four hours later Sonta comes into our hotel room. She is thinner and walks like she is injured, dragging her left leg: a big hematoma seems to hamper her knee.

Sitting on the edge of the bed, she looks at us but doesn't see us anymore. She has the look of an autistic child. Her body hides a spirit that seems to be off in another world. The old cotton towel slips from her little shoulders. Signs of lacerations show on her skinny back where she was beaten with a belt or a whip. A greenish liquid seeps from big red sores. Her pubis is swollen from a round brown mark: a large cigarette burn. I know this kind of wound very well now. Toy pours iced tea into a big glass; she drinks it in little sips, grimacing with pain. I examine her little mouth carefully. Her mouth is so full of abscesses, they form one big sore. This is a common infection in child prostitutes caused from lack of hygiene, repeated infections and fellations. Sonta is sleeping now and Toy sits on the window sill in silence. We cannot take our eyes off her. Her body, wrapped in the white cotton sheet, seems to have already left this life.

We cannot ignore the truth: Sonta is in distress. Sick, exhausted, she is going to die in this brothel if we don't get her out of here quickly.

We know the orders for security by heart. They can be summed up in a few words: no direct medical care of the children, no attempt to rescue them and no visits alone in the hotels. These minimum measures were discussed six months earlier at the time of our first meeting at the Camly Vietnamese Restaurant.

But this time we have reached a deadlock. I am not going to leave this place without having tried to get Sonta out of this brothel.

The rest? I have already told it: the discussion with Toy, his agreement in the end, how I affronted the fat Chinese, the negotiation, the deal made for eight hundred dollars, the child we took away, the doubt, the fear that they would take her back from us, how I went back into the hotel, and the Chinese boss's answer: "You have paid. Now get out!" And then, freedom for Sonta, and us, crazy with joy and worry, running down the street clutching this dying phantom of a child to us. Never, never will we let her go back to that hell!

We jump in a taxi and head for the home of our Thai friends. The little girl has fallen asleep on Toy's shoulder, the picture of a father and daughter. Incredible... We have bought a little girl, a human being, for a few thousand francs: the price of an expensive dog in one of those specialized shops in Brussels or Paris.

Sonta is welcomed very warmly by our friends. The problem is that she has no more reaction. She sits on the chaise longue for hours without moving. The children play around her. Her face shows no emotion. A red ball bounces on the back of her chair, but she doesn't even raise her head. I have the impression that a stone wall separates her from our world. I put her under the shower. She sits on the floor and lets the water run over her body for a long time. Later on, wearing a little green dress and plastic shoes, Sonta looks like all little Thai girls her age. The difference is inside. The other children play with dolls and listen to fairy tales. She, Sonta, has been raped and tortured like the worst of whores.

A friend of Toy's, a doctor in a private clinic, comes to examine the child. She prescribes a series of salves for the burns and infected sores. There are many cuts but nothing serious. After making a thorough examination, her face darkens. All at once she stops speaking English and begins to speak to Toy in Thai. I am beginning to understand the language, but I still cannot grasp everything. Contrary to the usual, Toy does not translate what she says. An icy silence fills the room. What is happening? Toy doesn't say anything.

A few days later we leave for Chiang-Mai in the northern region of Thailand to try and find Sonta's family. Two months ago she gave us the name of a village. Investigators from the Children's Center think they have found it about 700 miles from Bangkok. The north of Thailand is a strange region which has had little benefit from the country's economic development. The tribes, spread out over the mountains, still live cut off from the world. Until recently, the growing of poppies and the commerce of opium were their main resources. Forced by the Americans, the Thai government attacked this gigantic traffic. Hundreds of pounds of drugs left - and still leave! - from here by many different pathways. Bangkok's prison is full even today of many foreigners sentenced from five to twenty-five years for having bought the white powder. Thai jails are terrible; drugs circulate in the prison courtyards where prisoners have come to "shoot" themselves with the end of a needle and an empty pen, blowing the dose into their veins. Fights are frequent and ill-treatment is part of the daily routine. It is not surprising if they die from an "accidental fall".

I have often visited the prison of Swan Phloo, the Immigration Office's prison. It is terribly similar to the one in the movie *Midnight Express*, which shocked Europe in the seventies. It is a plain building with four floors and two sections of prisoners: two tiny rooms where sometimes almost two hundred people live in conditions of nonexistent hygiene. There are fewer women and therefore they have a little more space. The children are imprisoned with their mothers until they reach the age of twelve. After that, only the boys are transferred to the men's section. And that is when the hell begins: abuse and rape. I particularly remember one little Asian girl, from Bangladesh or the Philippines, ten or twelve years old, who banged her head against the walls, tore her hair our in bunches and screamed like a wounded animal. That was two years ago, during my first visit to Thailand. It took us four days to obtain permission from the local authorities and her embassy to transfer her to a hospital.

To find Sonta's family, Teelapon begins working from the office of the Center for the Protection of Children. He contacts many associations in the north and has a message transmitted over the radio: a missing person's bulletin for a little girl "found in the street" which gives Sonta's description. Teelapon hopes that someone in the village, a parent or a friend, will recognize the description of Sonta and contact the radio operators. There are many villages and they are too far apart to visit them all. If this doesn't work, the only thing we can do is turn her over to an orphanage. But in the condition she is in, I prefer not to think about this.

The first message, translated into four dialects, will be transmitted tonight on the mountain station. If someone should recognize Sonta from the description, they will still need the time it takes to descend to the town of Metchai, which is a four to six hour walk from the nearest villages, plus two or three hours by car to reach the asphalt road. The radio messages will be repeated all week. In the meantime, Toy will contact Yake, a village Chief of the Aka tribe and an active member of the Children's Foundation. He is known for his fight against the traffic of children. All by himself, Yake has already saved scores of little girls from prostitution. He knows the mountains like his own pocket. Yake is an ex border fighter who was close to the rebel chiefs for many long years. Today, Yake the rebel has ceased all subversive activity to fight against the capital's job agencies that wrest children from their families. He is a solitary man of the mountain who has decided to bar the Mafia's way all by himself. I am anxious to meet him. They say that he is the most important and the most respected of all the tribal Chiefs. He has three wives that live with him under the same roof. Their rank is determined by the amount of gold they have... on their teeth. At least they can't make a mistake.

The bus trip went fine. Sonta slept for several hours. When she awoke, her face seemed less somber. She even gave me her first smile. With her nose glued to the window, she watches the mountainous countryside pass by. A fine rain falls and the noise of the watter underneath the bus lulls us for the last few miles.

The bus pulls into the station of Chiang-Maï. As we get off, passengers hurry to pick up their cumbersome baggage. The bus leaves to continue its route toward Chiang-Rai, near the border with Burma.

Everything here is different from Bangkok. The climate is milder and a light breeze cools the air already warm for the month of March. This city seems calmer, more friendly. Tourists come here looking for the excitement of going into the jungle, the pleasure of hiking and riding around on an elephant's back. Sonta waits for some little sign of recognition from the mountains to the north.

We go to a local hotel: a wooden building by the river that has a dozen rooms with bamboo furniture and mosquito nets draped over the beds. The bathroom can be summed up as a small room with a rough floor and a huge earthenware jar of rain water. There is a message for us at the reception desk. Toy rushes to the telephone. Good news at last! Two families have called the local radio. They think they recognize their daughter from the description of Sonta. I hope that one of the two is the right one. We will leave for Chiang-Rai tomorrow to meet the radio announcer and look for the family. We decide to visit the closest village having a name that phonetically sounds like the name Sonta gave us. To get there, we will hike ten hours on dusty trails under a burning sun. I doubt that I can make it. I don't know yet that in the coming years I will walk hundreds of miles in this region under the burning sun and pouring rain.

A three hour bus ride takes us to the city of Chiang-Rai. There are fewer tourists here. Cattle raising and agriculture allow the population to subsist far from the busy capital with its concrete monsters and its brothels.

Atchou is a young man of about twenty. He is waiting for us at the local radio station. He is small with very dark skin, wears traditional dress and a big half-moon smile; he is very very nice. We spend the day at the home of a friend of his, an old man over seventy, as we would say in Brussels. The old man meets us at the door of his wood house. His bones stand out under the dark brown skin of his skinny body. The inside of the little house is like the treasure cave of Ali Baba with dozens of sculptured wooden objects and woven baskets all around the floor. We sit down on a floor mat while the old man prepares hot tea. And then... a miracle! For the first time in ages Sonta speaks. In the beginning, just a few inarticulate sounds, then the sound of bells: laughter. Her laughter! The old man smiles and continues the conversation in Sonta's dialect. The mountains and sights from the past have given her the strength to come out of her shell. Chance does not exist, luck is with us! Now I am sure that we will find her family.

Toy has come back with information, a map and a route to guide us on the dirt paths. He has also bought some provisions: dried fish, some cereal, dried fruit and a big cotton blanket because the nights are cool up here!

Sonta talks a little with Toy before falling asleep on a blanket. The men keep watch most of the night by the light of an oil lamp. I fall asleep under the stars, lulled by the crackling of the radio and the hum of crickets. We leave the old man at dawn promising to stop on our way back. This magician who gave back the power to speak to Sonta deserves this homage!

Sonta is beaming. She is wearing red cotton overalls, a ribbon in her hair and a colored knapsack on her back. The trip by taxi bus lasts three hours. We are jolted back and forth by the holes in the road just like the farmers who are on their way to the city to sell their produce.

The bus stops. Now the long march begins. The little girl is already far ahead. She walks briskly in front of us without even looking back. What a beautiful sight! Not long ago Sonta was still a living corpse; now, in a hurry to get back home, she prances at the head of our little group picking wild flowers here and there, and sometimes she comes back from a bend in the path to give us a beautiful smile.

As we walk, we are torn between happiness and worry. What if this is not the right family? And what if there is no one to take care of her? Enough. Grandmother Simm would have said, "We don't get anywhere with "ifs".

Night has fallen. We have walked many hours without stopping. We have passed men and women bent over planting tea or corn. They all wear traditional clothes made from brightly colored cloth woven by hand, metallic headdresses with little round bells and intricately worked silver jewelry. Time has stopped. There is no electricity here, only oil lamps. Information is passed from mouth to mouth. The local radio transmits only a few hours a day.

Every now and then we see straw huts and smoke from cooking fires. We can also hear children singing and screaming. A few hundred yards more and we will be able to set down our rucksacks for the night.

This village consists of a dozen wooden houses built on stilts. There is only one floor, a large platform for a family of ten to twenty people. Not to mention the pigs, chickens and dogs that live on the ground level.

The village chief's son shows us to a house available for the night. The men have gone off to the mountain to work, probably in one of the opium plantations hidden along the border with Burma. Later we will cross other villages where there are no adults, all gone for many months. As we walk, we encounter mules bearing baskets that seem full to bursting. These good animals know the way so well, they walk without a guide. The mountain says that these mules transport dried opium flowers. But shh! This subject is taboo here. Better to respect it.

A woman welcomes us very kindly. She spreads mats on the floor. Sonta goes to sleep fully dressed. The flame from the oil lamp dances for a long time on the wooden walls before dying in the moonless night.

A new day begins. We still have six hours to walk before reaching the village that could be Sonta's. We leave early to take advantage of the cool hours of the day. At eleven o'clock, the heat becomes oppressive and we are forced to rest under a tree. End of our break; now we must recuperate the time lost. Sonta climbs the winding path with the agility of people from the mountains. Sometimes she is so far ahead all we can see are the colors of her backpack. Toy can walk for many hours in total silence, his expression fixed on the horizon.

One last effort: there are still two more miles to go to reach the village Sonta is hoping for. Children are watching us from their perches in the trees and communicate with each other with little wooden whistles. Occasionally we can hear their laughter.

Sonta walks faster, then starts running as fast as she can, shouting, laughing and crying. Children surround her and help her to climb the extremely steep pathway even faster. She seems to be carried by the wind.

A woman is waiting at the top of the hill, her face wet with tears. Sonta throws herself into the woman's arms and their entwined bodies become one, that of a mother and her child. Toy takes hold of my hand and we walk the last few yards of the trail together. Women are crying. Children are pushing to see the little girl better, men are talking in loud voices. Only the old people watch this incredible scene in silence. Toy and I withdraw from the crowd and sit down on a freshly cut tree trunk savoring this moment that we have hoped for so much! Something resounds inside me, like the clang of an enormous bell at Easter time, something much louder that the noise of room keys or screaming from a porno video or the cries of a child being abused, something like fantastic music, with words, always the same, simple yet wonderful words: "Sonta has come home!"

We have one night left, just one, to complete the rescue: tell her family the truth, tell them how and where their daughter has lived, convince them to accept her and, no matter what, not to reject her. See to it that between Sonta and her mother, between the re-formed family and the community, the reunion is complete. The village chief approaches. He is about fifty, skin browned by the sun and the rough hands of a man who works the soil. Custom imposes that he host passing strangers in his home. He has an immense house raised on four stilts. Woven mats cover the floor. Baskets, tools, a weapon, bags of seed and dried plants sit on the floor. There is no furniture, neither table nor chair. They live, sleep and eat on the mats. The chief's wife is sitting in a corner of the room with a small baby in her arms. She supervises her four daughters as they prepare the meal. An old woman with a skeletal body chews tobacco.

We sit down on the platform around a tray of green tea. The chief pours boiling water into goblets made of bamboo. Several men, Sonta's relatives, and some adolescents stand around watching us with curiosity. A little girl comes to touch my blond hair and runs away laughing. Being a foreigner, the men stare at me. I must be the first one to come to their village. I am not a tourist looking for adventure like they encounter sometimes, but a Westerner accompanied by a Thai who has brought a child back to them: a little Aka girl. The chief thanks us over and over for this deed. Hesitatingly, he hands me a small piece of cloth in which is wrapped an old piece of silver that shines with a patina that comes only from time. This coin is the symbol of Sonta's story. I will keep it with me always.

Serious discussions can now begin. For hours the men talk with Toy in their dialect. Everything is explained to them: the details of the first meeting and the situation of the children in Bangkok's brothels. Toy talks a lot and shows them pictures. The people from the village stare wide-eyed with horror, rooted to the spot. They take us back in time.

It was a morning in November eighteen months ago. Five children play on the red dirt trail where they always go sliding down the slope on their wooden wagons. A red and white pick-up truck stops: such a vehicle is rarely seen here. A city woman with braided hair and wearing a green silk dress gets out. The girls think she is very pretty. She asks them for directions and chats with the children. A man joins her and hands out plastic balloons. Pretty yellow balloons. "Not like the ones our old folks make with pieces of straw!" says a young boy sitting to my right. The little girls go closer to the truck. Then everything happens very fast: a man's hands grab three children, the door closes and the truck takes off in a cloud of dust. It's like a bad film. For a few moments, the two boys who were not taken are paralyzed with fear. Then they run to give the alarm, but at that time of the morning the village is empty. Only the old people, too tired to go to the fields, are sitting on the terraces. Several minutes pass before the adults are alerted. Too much time has been lost. The pick-up truck is already far away. Three little girls have disappeared: Sonta, six years old; Pramun, eleven and Moodame, eight.

Sonta continues the story: in the truck, a piece of wet cotton is pressed over her nose. After that? She doesn't remember anything. Only that she cannot keep her eyes open and sleeps soundly. When she wakes up, she is alone in the office of a job agency. A man comes in, comes over to her and closely examines her body, her feet and her teeth. Standing in front of this stranger, Sonta thinks of how the farmers in the village examine a buffalo before buying it. There is something similar in the man's eyes that evening. When the stranger leaves the room, she still does not know that her next stop is a children's brothel in Bangkok: the Suriwongse Hotel.

In the village, they say that children occasionally disappear in the mountains. But they say so many things sitting around in the evenings. Right after the disappearance, the chief and the fathers of the children went down from the mountain to the nearest police station, several hours by foot. The officer told them that the chance of finding their children was very slight: Bangkok has a population of six million. He typed a declaration that the men from the tribe signed with an X. Since then, Aka children are not allowed to play outside the limits of the village. The mothers cried a lot, the seasons passed, the red and white pick-up truck never returned, and the children were never seen again. At dawn the next day, the chief tells us about another Aka community three hours away where other children have disappeared.

Evidently the region has become a reservoir of children for the procurers. The northern part of the country is cut off from the rest of the world. The tribes live in perfect autarky, no one knows how to read or write and these country people easily believe the stories of city people.

Night has fallen on the village like a black veil. The sky is studded with stars, the kerosene lamp begins to go out. We have talked for a long time. Tonight Sonta will sleep in her mother's arms. Contrary to our fears, the members of the tribe never had the least word of condemnation for the little ex-prostitute; her mother will never stop hugging her re-found daughter. Our worries were unfounded: these mountain people have the intelligence that comes from the heart. This is a magic night.

And yet, by the light of the kerosene lamp, I see sadness on Toy's face, and I cannot understand why. What could ruin the success of this day? We have become very close to one another. We can tell each other everything. Or almost. For the last few days, I have had the feeling that he is hiding something serious from me. I want to ask him but he stops me with a sign of his hand and takes me by the arm, comes close to my cheek and whispers: "Sonta is HIV positive."

I want to scream, but my voice won't come. Faces flash through my mind: the kids of the Suriwongse, the fat Chinese, Alain the architect and all the others. So the crocodiles kill, too. First they steal the children's childhood, then they torture them, and in the end they murder them. I cannot stand the idea that Sonta is going to die in the near future. I can still see her lying on the dingy bed in room 224. She looked so fragile. Now, back with her own people, she seemed to be protected against her past. Sonta is HIV positive! AIDS! No, no and no! It can't be possible! Not her, not now!

Toy had the courage to talk to the village chief about this disease, the first signs, the risk of contamination, a small brown mark on the girl's thigh, the abscesses in her mouth, the list of symptoms that will indicate the advancement of the disease in Sonta's body. I doubt that AIDS means very much in this tribe in the mountains, but I prefer to know that Sonta is here, surrounded by her people, rather than alone and isolated in a hospital in Bangkok.

Toy is silent, but I know he is not sleeping. The two of us wait for dawn.

At five a.m. the children are already squabbling around the fountain. Sonta is among them, playing with her brothers and sisters as if she had never left the village. It is time to get moving. Five hours later we see the other village hanging on the side of a red dirt hill. Four children have disappeared from this village: two boys, ten and eleven, and two girls, eight and nine. It happened seven months ago. The scenario is exactly the same: a pick-up truck, a woman who lures the children and kidnaps them in less than two minutes. After that there is no news of them.

Each family describes their lost child. Toy takes notes and shows them pictures of children we have seen in the hotels. We promise to keep after the police in Bangkok when we return and to refer every case to the Center for the Protection of Children. What else can we do? We don't have a single clue.

We leave for Bangkok the next day at dawn. We must continue our investigation in the brothels to learn more about who is behind this traffic. We know now who the victims are: children from the tribes in the north, Chinese and Burmese minors. I also want to take the time to get to know the consumers, the false tourists who go unpunished for rape, because I am convinced that the demand creates the offer in this category. How can I accept the idea that Sonta is going to die of AIDS, contaminated by some bastard who continues along his merry way? I can see him in some chic spot in Paris or anywhere else, a parlor crocodile, speaking about new love and the pleasure given to the children. We have "crocodile authors" in the West. They publish pretty books about their experiences with little children. They are never accused, never sent for psychiatric treatment, never forbidden to go near children. No, in the name of literature, we give them the floor for as long as they want.

12.

HUNTING DOWN THE "CROCODILES"

I now know that it is possible to encounter pedophiles in certain hotels. Leaning on the bar, drunk "crocodiles" talk easily about their long experience in Thailand or the charms of Saigon. To learn more, the best places are, without a doubt, the breakfast rooms of shady hotels. There, in the morning, most of these "tourists" have one thing in common, regardless of their age or nationality: they slept with a child the night before. To continue our investigation, we now want to study more closely these individuals who travel five thousand miles to rent a child.

An investigation with scientific pretensions would have to cover a longer period of time, but our financial means will not permit it. Furthermore, I am beginning to doubt my personal ability to endure such horrors much longer. We have forty-five days, or rather forty-five nights, to gather as much information as possible.

Pattaya seems to be the best point of observation, so we decide to spend a week there. Our method is simple: stay in a guest house and hang around the bars and on the beach all night. Little by little we begin to comprehend how the system works. Every night is the same. Children from seven to fourteen are on the lookout for an easy little job hoping to get a few bahts or, better, a bed for the night. They end up in the back room of bars. So it's the night spots that furnish little kids to their customers. The bars have become the point of encounter for demand and offer, the waiting room, the selection center. The deal is clear: the customers find what they are looking for, the boss makes a profit. As for the kids... the youngest, forsaken, seek contact with the adults hoping to get a little money out of them and maybe a little affection, a major note the pedophiles play to get close to the children. This beach resort two hours away from Bangkok has everything to supply the market for crocodiles: miserable kids, sun and beaches, scores of bars run by accomplice procurers and a "blind" police. Pattaya is a city without a soul.

Very soon we discover a strange residence for rich retired Westerners. Hiding in one of the building's darkest entrances, we have been watching this place for two nights now. A Thai regularly delivers little boys about ten years old to the tenants. The children arrive in groups of four around ten-thirty p.m. and leave the building early in the morning. This merry-go-round seems to be repeated every evening. Always the same group of children, sometimes accompanied by a few adolescents, depending on the request. Among these children I recognize two who, not long ago, were sleeping on the beach huddled against a dune. One of the two, the youngest, was holding a bag of glue in his hand.

During the day, no one could imagine that this traffic exists. Elderly people between sixty and eighty stroll leisurely in the park next to this building on the beach front. An elderly American man walks here every day, hand in hand with a young adolescent. There is no doubt about the nature of their relationship.

One morning, we decide we will approach one of these children as he comes out of the building. Around five-thirty, a little boy comes through the door. He is ten years old at the most, wears green shorts and a Michael Jackson T-shirt. Standing barefooted on the sidewalk, he doesn't seem to know where to go, hesitates for a while, then goes toward the beach. We follow him. The boy sits on the sand and looks at the horizon. Two bills of five hundred bahts are sticking out of the back pocket of his shorts.

Toy goes up to him. A few words is all it takes to gain his trust. These children are desperately vulnerable. Tchoum is ten and a half, has a round face and shiny black eyes. His story is a classical one: he is the oldest in a family of three children.   There is no father and the twenty-seven-year-old mother is a prostitute in a local bar. Tchoum ran away to the world of the streets. For almost two years the boy has been living in the network of old, foreign pedophiles. Every year, during the good season, they come to stay for three to six months in this deluxe building in the high-class district of Pattaya. Tchoum says he is lucky, his customer is always the same: a very old English man "with the skin of a crocodile," says the boy making a face. The English man asks the child to leave the building every morning at dawn and to come back when it's dark. Or to spend the night somewhere else, depending on his mood. Salary: a bed, a shower, something to eat and the equivalent of a hundred francs.   In three days we counted fifteen boys like Tchoum.   Their "contact" is the barman of the Mairmaid; all the old pedophiles have to do is give the password, a strange phrase that everyone in the building knows: "I want a night on the deserted mountain." The Mairmaid, a bar similar to hundreds of others in Pattaya, is the bar this clientele prefers. Just like everywhere else, there are tourists with pale faces and some girls wiggling to bad music. At the far end of the room, little boys watch for a sign from the "contact" who quickly takes them away in his pick-up.

I decide that I want to talk to one of these elderly pedophiles. Tomorrow we will go look for them.

Four-thirty p.m. Clouds hide the sun, the ocean is gray and the tourists begin to leave the beach.   Nearby, our American is lying comfortably on a chaise longue. To his right the body of an adolescent is stretched out on a colored beach towel. The man and the young Thai get up, go into the water and swim in the waves. The old man embraces the boy. I wait until they leave the beach before approaching. Suddenly the old man becomes aware of us. My face must betray my feelings.

I walk up to them and introduce myself as an assistant at the Children's Center. Toy begins a conversation with the young boy. The old man's reaction is quite surprising. He seems like an animal caught in a trap. He threatens to call the police. It appears that we are on private property! Toy steps in. Coldly he tells the man that we have proof of his pedophilia. The tone of his voice leaves no room for denial. The man sits down on a bench as if he feels sick.

Unknown to him, we record the conversation: a ninety-minute confession by a man who has been abusing children in the United States and everywhere else he went for business since he was thirty-five. At the age of twelve he was raped by a teacher in his boarding school. As an adult he created his own logic. Later on we listen to the tape again, analyzing what he said and dissecting his arguments: his thoughts are just a monolithic block. Not a single one of our arguments could make him change his way of thinking. The main ideas are always the same: "new love", the authenticity of these adult/child relationships, the children's sense of seduction, and, of course, the "famous" Asiatic culture that authorizes this form of love. He doesn't rape children: he offers them pleasure. In his heart, he loves them. Don't confuse this with what his teacher made him suffer!

He has been coming to Thailand for almost seven years and stays six months. He doesn't have to worry about the laws here, everything is possible with a few hundred dollars. We leave this pervert sitting on the bench. A few days later, his apartment is up for rent. A brief moment of conscience or flight to another "crocodile" paradise?

At the Punky Bar, Baby Bar and Mamaya, the decor, girls, music, and customers are strangely the same. Perhaps Nicolas, a rather good-looking Swiss guy in his thirties, is a little different from the others. He has the relaxed face of someone who sleeps at night, expensive clothes and long curly hair carefully tied with a leather string. His accent is distinctly French Swiss. We pick him out of the usual crowd right away. A lost tourist? No, he speaks a few words of Thai, knows the customers and the girls: too much for a simple tourist. We approach the bar. Nicolas notices us. We start talking; the conversation is going to last four hours. Under the effect of alcohol and a few joints, we are going to discover the very special course of a thirty-year-old pedophile.

In Switzerland, Nicolas is, or rather was, a teacher in a private school in the Canton of Vaud. He left to go to Asia for eighteen months to work for a welfare organization in the shanty towns. He tells us about a school built of bamboo and his French lessons in a Bangkok ghetto. His story seems a little odd to me: they don't teach French in the shanty towns of the capital! Nicolas's story is very vague. Obviously he is not telling me the truth and remains secretive about the school where he taught in Switzerland. He left his country for a reason, but what? He won't say. The fact remains that he landed here with enough money to live for several months lounging on the beaches close to the children of Pattaya where a cheap hotel costs sixty francs a night and a kid from the street barely the price of a good meal. He lights a third joint.

Nicolas says that here he experiences "complete love" with very young girls but also with young boys picked up off the street. The average age of these conquests varies between twelve and fifteen. He knows where to find children in good health as well as the others, those that inhale glue. Reluctantly, he tells us about a bar that supplies boys seven to twelve years old. Nicolas has always had sexual relationships with children. First in Switzerland, where as a teacher he would go to swimming pools and draw kids into the locker room or to his house:

- They are budding lovers. What I love with the children is the contact of their small mouth on my sex. I don't rape anyone because I never penetrate them. Or at least not the first time. I never force them. I never hit them. Not like a lot of other people!

Nicolas confirms that bruises from beatings, cuts and cigarette burns are inflicted not only by the brothel keepers but come from violence by the "crocodiles" too. Later on I will have the opportunity to verify that some pedophiles come all the way to Thailand to play the sadist with children. All they have to do is pay the hotel manager or the floor boy a little more. In Europe this is called "extreme cruelty to children" and those found guilty serve long prison terms.

- In Switzerland I was always afraid. Afraid of the women who always leave me one day for someone else. Afraid of jail and the metal bars they put people like me behind in the name of their holy morals. Here, nothing in the behavior of the police or the authorities makes us think that this is illegal. We have money. They leave us alone.

Twice on the tape recorded without his knowledge, Nicolas repeats that he doesn't hurt the children, that he needs them to go on living and that he, too, was loved by an adult. Loved, abused or raped when he was a little boy? It doesn't matter. Since then, armed with his good conscience, a little money, the instructions-for-use of Pattaya-the-whore and a cheap philosophy on "new love", he can treat himself every night, without remorse and without risk, to kids that consider him a "crocodile" and leave early in the morning with the urge to vomit. Nicolas the teacher is blind. Because it's in his interest.

This is our last night in the bars before going back to Bangkok. We are beginning to look like the local tourists: the lack of sleep, forced drinking of sweet sodas and alcohol and the depressing sights at night have given us the same muddy coloring and the same sad look. Tonight we are making our last investigation in one of these "fly-by-night" bars. That has become our nickname for this particular kind of bar because they are made of four wooden boards: a central room and a cardboard partition in front of which the tourists clump together. We walk on the beach in the direction of a wooden hut. Three green lamps mark the spot for consumers. Here, depraved males touch bottom. These are the lowest-level brothels.

Two tourists, drunk on Mékong whiskey, sleep leaning against the wooden façade. The smell of beer, sweat and garbage hits us in the stomach. A few men are wiggling to the rhythm of Thai music. In the back, a disgusting-looking German tourist pushes a very young wire-thin girl behind the partition. The music stops and a bunch of German tourists begin beating their hands together. I don't understand. Toy wants to leave. Absolutely not. I want to know what is going on. All at once everything is silent again. The big German reappears, sweating, red and half undressed. He pushes the proof of his exploitation in front of him: the teenager, naked to the waist, her face marked with humiliation. I walk out like a robot. Bending over the sand, I vomit. From shame.

A man comes out of the bar and asks in French if I need help. I tell him I am sick from the drinks. He smells of alcohol, too. He sits down on the sand. French, young, a normal face with fine features. What is he doing in this dive? He has just left a fifteen-year-old girl and he feels bad, horrible, guilty. He is head of the sales department in a French-German firm in Stuttgart; he has two daughters, ten and fifteen. And now he has done it with a girl the same age as one of his daughters. His office colleagues clapped for him too. This is too much for tonight. I want to go back to the hotel and sleep until tomorrow when I can leave this place. I hate the hypocrisy of this city, its vendors of children and its Western buyers. I hate their networks, their circuits. I hate this business, its tranquil banality.

I was blind. I had hoped to find monsters, devourers of children, bellowing ogres, not men with white skin and courteous manners, not these Mr. Anyone, not my neighbor! I'm angry. Bewildered. Somewhere else, in another context, I must have already met them, had pleasant conversations, even become acquainted. But friends? No! I will never agree. Toy tries to soothe my bitterness, repeating that this man is not typical of what we came to see. Toy is right, of course, but for tonight, I don't want to listen. I have seen too much.

Bus No. 12 speeds toward Bangkok. Tomorrow is Sunday and by my own authority, I give myself a day off. I plan to visit the week-end market and spend an afternoon by the swimming pool. John is away again. We communicate through our answering machines. His beautiful apartment is the link of our meetings in Asia. Chem, the housekeeper, is not there anymore. She has gone back to the northeast to be with her family. That's too bad, I liked her very much. I have to get going. This day is going to be too short.

We still have to verify a good dozen addresses of brothels found in international guidebooks and two "massage" centers up north. Tonight we are going to meet at Sowit's bar, the prostitute whose four fingers were cut off. Sowit wants to help us. She has a friend who knows an interesting French customer who comes here four or five times a year. He doesn't look for adult prostitutes, but for small girls. Sowit's friend thinks that the children are photographed for the catalog of a travel agency in France. She knows a child prostitute around Suriwongse Road who has posed nude for this stranger several times, alone or performing with an adult.

A few weeks ago, a Thai travel agency in connection with a French tour agent asked a dozen children to go to the airport to welcome some tourists. The deal was clear: one hundred francs a day, meals and room with the tourist. A little boy went to welcome a stranger at the airport, a man about forty, a *phareng*, as they call Europeans here. The adult and the child spent a week together in a luxury hotel.

It is still early. Toy insists that we go see the vendors of snake blood and the Chinese gymnasts at Lumpini park.

In this last green spot in the center of town, vendors of "magic potions" can still be seen on the week-ends. Little shops display bamboo goblets that contain real snake blood. Chinese tradition holds that this potion holds the secret of youth. Further along, old women in black costumes are practicing slow airy gymnastics. The new generation prefers to build big muscles in body-building gyms. By the lake, Thai families have come to spend the day; parents are already preparing lunch, children argue over a ball. Sitting on a bench, we watch the way these small people live. They probably don't know very much about what happens to the kids of Patpong.

It is time to get back to the bar where we are going to meet Sowit's prostitute friend. She is standing in front of the Pink Panther, a show bar where foreigners stand in line to get in. This evening, she looks like a typical Thai woman: elegantly dressed and little make-up. It is hard to imagine her as a gogo girl who dances half naked while the tourists watch. Because that is what she has been doing for the last two years. Her story is a mystery. She refuses to talk about it. We respect her wishes. We have a meeting with her young friend in a small restaurant about ten minutes from the hot section of town. He is already there, at table No. 13, his face hidden by the menu. There is no question about it:

he cannot be more than twelve years old. The boy tells us his story while eating hot shrimp soup.

He was born poor in one of the capital's shanty towns. He grew up with a violent alcoholic father who one day disappeared. His mother collects trash to sell to the ragmen from the "smoking mountain" of Ladprao. One day a man passed through the shanty town's narrow muddy alleys. He was looking for children for a travel agency: a week's work in exchange for a room, rice every day and a little money. The boy left without leaving even a trace behind him. After that, in the tourist section of town, the same man passes regularly to offer him the same kind of work: one week, three weeks sometimes, with foreigners in one of the hotels in Bangkok, Pattaya or Pukket.

The boy says he doesn't like this kind of work but it is easy and very well-paying. Except that the foreigners are strange and always want him to masturbate them, caress them and sometimes "do things that hurt." The boy recognized his own picture in a *phareng's* album. There are many pictures of small nude boys in the catalog for tourists. That's all. Toy translated word for word.

Unfortunately, none of his information can help us locate the contact or the travel agency. We will have to use the child as bait. But is it worth it to distess him further to prove that this traffic exists? His testimony confirms what we already know.

We decide to take the boy to the Foundation's social service. Toy assures me that they can put him in one of the projects under way. He calls the Foundation and in less than an hour one of their social assistants meets us. A protection home has already accepted to take charge of him. Finally, talk that has led to a concrete solution. To ascertain a child's slavery without being able to immediately do anything about it is the most difficult thing I know. I feel more vulnerable at every new encounter. That's all for tonight. We say good-night on the sidewalk.

I return to John's apartment. He really has exquisite taste, a talent for finding superb objects during his travels in Asia. What a strange person he is, however. We are so close to each other and yet hardly know one another. When he was director of the projects, we worked together with refugees at the border. After that, we communicated by mail. One day in February I received a strange letter from Hong Kong: two pages of blue paper with incomprehensible phrases scribbled in twirling handwriting. One of these phrases asks me to forgive him:

- Forgive me for deceiving you, forgive me for lying.

The letter was signed John. And that is certainly my name on the envelope. I don't understand. When he returned, John refused to talk about it, but this letter has remained a black spot in our relationship. Why did he say he deceived me?

13.

DINNER AT THE ORIENTAL HOTEL

It is finally Sunday, my day off! I'm off to the swimming pool at the Oriental Hotel. A lovely afternoon... until my gaze lights on a face I know. Alain, the French architect I met at the Suriwongse during the first phase of our investigation, is sitting right there in front of us. Smiling. Apparently he hasn't forgotten us. In a flash, I see again the dirty images of the Suriwongse and Sonta's face. Toy throws me a questioning look... O.K.! Let's go take up the game again with this Frenchman, father of a family, follower of the theory of "new love." Back to work.

Alain has been in Thailand almost three weeks now and in a few days he will be returning to Lyon, where he lives with his wife and children. This trip has been similar to preceding ones: a building contract in Thailand and a week at the Suriwongse Hotel where he slept with a few little boys. After that, he went to the best hotel in Bangkok to receive his collaborators and clients. Some nights, he slips quickly over to the hot section of town to find a child at random on the street. He takes the child to a hotel used by prostitutes, then later returns to his luxury hotel to sleep. The child is left to sleep on the sidewalk of some main street, preferably under a street lamp so he won't be attacked by other kids.

I accept Alain's invitation to dinner at the Oriental Hotel, which overlooks the river. It is a little after eight. Soft music is playing to the light of paper lanterns and large colored candles. There is something magic about the place. Sitting on a white rattan sofa in his superb Armani suit with a beautiful tie painted with Van Gogh's famous sunflowers and wearing gold colored glasses, Mr. Alain is really the perfect example of an elegant company director. When he speaks, he chooses his words. Once in a while he blots his forehead with a silk handkerchief embroidered with his initials. I am scared to death that he has seen through my game and I don't have the courage to discretely turn on my tape recorder. Too bad. Anyway, I will never forget a single word of this conversation. Toy preferred not to come so I could be alone with my "compatriot," as he says. I decided that if I have to, I'll put my cards on the table. Alain smiles at me:

- I am very glad you accepted my invitation to dinner this evening. But then again, I suggested it the first time we met, didn't I? Ah! but that was several months ago... Let's see... It was at the Suriwongse Hotel. Am I right?

- Exactly. In the breakfast room. You had spent the night with a ten-year-old boy. You said that he had given you much pleasure. And we talked about the philosophy of "new love..."

I attacked immediately. At least we were on the subject.

- What a memory! To tell the truth, I don't remember exactly what I told you in that horrible dining room. I prefer this setting by far. The Suriwongse is a strange place... A kind of place for debauchery and perdition where people like me can take a break to have love relations with a child.

Well, one thing is sure: Alain still talks frankly. He continues:

- In a few hours, we can live off all the fantasies accumulated over the months. I am lucky to be able to come to this country three or four times a year. I can free myself of these... terrible ...urges.

- Terrible?...

- ... Because we are victims of a self-righteous society. We love children with a love spelled with a capital 'L'. Every single day, when I am in France, just seeing a little girl or boy leaves me with a violent feeling of frustration. I need to touch them, feel their skin. That beautiful skin, like peaches covered with a light fuzz They shiver under my fingers. No woman in the world can give me the same sensation. None.

The waiter brings our order. A bellboy from the hotel walks around carrying a poster inviting a Mr. Hasashi to come to the reception desk. A Japanese gets up from the table beside us. I am not hungry. I must continue:

- Tell me, Alain... If I remember correctly, you told me you had a family, a wife... Isabelle, right?... and young children. I picture you with a beautiful wife from a well-to-do family in Lyon, a house straight out of an interior decorating magazine, full of rare objects bought during your travels in Asia. Am I right?

He bursts out laughing:

- That's incredible! How could you remember all those details? You described my surroundings exactly.

- That's not surprising. You said it would be hard to imagine yourself married to a supermarket cashier in a low-rent district in the suburbs.

He smiles, flattered.

- In fact my wife is very beautiful, a brilliant upper-class girl I met during the last year of my studies to become an architect. We got married very quickly. My first daughter was born one year later. Typical, no? Isabelle hates to travel, she would much rather visit with her parents in Brittany. Isa belongs to only one man, the kind of woman it is impossible to leave because there is nothing you can criticize about her.

- Many men would love to be in your shoes. However, I don't think I'm wrong when I say that if you are here, it's because something in you... you... how can I say?

He interrupts me:

- Yes, I see what you mean. You know, money can't buy everything. I'll be frank: I had what is called a happy childhood, a very good education, wonderful parents, brothers and sisters to get into mischief with and a lot of friends. I went to a religious boarding school for ten years. I can remember it as if it were yesterday. I boarded at the school and came home twice a month. In the beginning, I loved that environment of fraternity that you find in all boys' schools.

- But?

- But one day... it was a Wednesday, I think... I was only eleven, maybe twelve... the gym teacher asked me if I wanted to work on my butterfly stroke. I had talent, really. So I went to practice, but I was surprised to see that I was the only pupil invited to work out. This teacher had the reputation of being severe but fair with his students. Once in the water, we went over the movements, and suddenly I felt a hand slide under my bathing suit and caress my sex. He looked at me, smiling with satisfaction. I didn't dare to say anything. He was the teacher. At the next lesson, he took me into the baby pool and lay on my back. I felt a terrible pain tear at my stomach. I couldn't move; his hand kept caressing my sex without stopping. Another time, he came into the locker room - my locker was always way in the back - he flattened me on the bench and started again. He hurt me. And he threatened to have me expelled from school if I told anyone about these special lessons. To be expelled from school would have been the worst thing for my father and would have disgraced my brothers, who were in the same school. I never told anyone. These special lessons lasted five years, every Wednesday, without exception. The teacher said that he loved me very much and that he had chosen me out of five hundred students. I got used to it, and I ended up loving this teacher and his caresses.

I remain silent. All he is is a child who has been sexually abused. Alain continues:

- When I was fifteen, my parents bought a house in the north of France. After we moved, I became a day student at the school. Sometimes I would think about those afternoons with my teacher, and then I would go to the pool and grab a boy of six, seven, nine, eleven, take him into the locker room and oblige him to touch me. Only once I had a problem with a boy seven years old, Raphael. He started screaming and I had just enough time to throw him out in the hall and close the door! Then I went to college and I had a couple of affairs there with guys my age. But what the hell... the thing I really love is the feel of small children. The smoothness of their skin. Their little tiny mouth. I am not a homosexual. I have made love with women, but I did it without pleasure, mechanically; I let them guide me... believe...

- You said that Isabelle is a brilliant woman. She must have felt there was something in you that wasn't right. That you were unhappy and that...

He interrupts me curtly:

- Isabelle wanted two children: she has them. Since then, we make love very rarely. And only when she insists, when she wants to prove that we are a real couple after she has read some article in *Marie-Claire!*

- Look, the problem is that you are unhappy...

He cuts in again:

- The problem isn't that I love little children; the problem is that our good French society doesn't allow this pleasure. In our country, when you love a child, they call it sexual abuse in the scandal papers. Me, I never hurt the kids. They masturbate me and I penetrate them only if they've already done it with others. Afterward, I give them money or I buy them presents. If I pick them up at a pool in France, I buy them something at the cafeteria. But I never rape them. Never!

Now he is on the defensive. I have to get back on his ground to find out more about the environment:

- You must have read a lot about new love?

He relaxes:

- Yes, I have read several books by authors who believe in this philosophy, in particular Gabriel Matzneff. And I regularly receive foreign magazines because I belong to some clubs. They are delivered to a post office box I have where I live. NAMBLA, North American Man-Boy Love Association, publishes some interesting things. I keep them at the office in a locked drawer.

It is time for me to be more direct. I question him:

- When your teacher touched you twenty-five years ago, was that abuse or love?

Silence. Alain asks for the desert menu without answering the question. After a moment, he notices that my plate is untouched:

- That's strange, Marie. You have jabbed every grain of soy on your dish with your fork, but you haven't eaten anything.

He notices everything. I don't think he trusts me. Now he is the one who asks the questions:

- Why did you agree to have dinner with me this evening? You remember every detail about our first meeting at the Suriwongse. You're looking for something, aren't you?

O.K. It's time to lay my cards on the table:

- Yes, I am trying to understand what brings you, and others like you, to touch children, with or without violence, just to appease the sex phantoms that you disguise behind a pretended philosophy. No, it's true, I am not a pedophile. I am investigating the prostitution of children in Bangkok. But don't worry, I'm not a cop either. You trusted me and I won't do anything to cause you trouble. You are ill, Alain. You need to have sexual relations with children, but more than anything, you need treatment. "New love" does not exist. It's all a big mistake. It's dangerous for the children. I met the little ten-year-old boy who caressed and masturbated you at the Suriwongse. Listen: he is a child prisoner and covered with sores. Didn't you see them, you who notices everything? He doesn't like what he does. He dreams about a family, a mother to kiss him good-night. A mother... not a stranger who touches him all night!

Alain is startled. Suddenly he loses his polite way of speaking:

- Cut it out! You don't know what you're saying! You're just another one of those hysterical fucking papists!

- I am not a Catholic, not a believer and not hysterical, and I love my husband physically just as he loves me!

At a table nearby, some French people turn to look at us. We look like a couple that is breaking up. Alain calls the waiter and demands the desert menu again. For a moment there, I thought he was going to ask for the bill and leave. I order ice cream with fruit, he orders cream puffs with chocolate sauce and English tea. The waiter disappears and the discussion begins again on the same tone:

- I can't see why the hell you are making this investigation nor what you are trying to find out! You are mixing two different cultures, opposite outlooks. And in the name of I don't know what moral, you want to protect kids that have love in them from when they are very young. You're on the wrong track. I say that Thai children are experts about this because it is part of their education. Here, parents teach children what love is, they touch them and allow them to discover their bodies and its pleasures. Fathers love their little daughters so much that they offer them their first experience of love!

- In what exotic film did you see this hogwash? I have been living here for years! Quit taking your desires for reality.

- My desires? You must be joking. In Europe, our daughters offer their virginity to strangers outside the family. I don't think it's a bit normal that a guy from I-don't-know-where makes love to my fifteen-year-old daughter for the first time. I could help her discover something fabulous through my feelings!

- This has a name: it's called incest. Did you do it, this "new love," with your children?

- No, it's against my wife's principles, against her "morals" and above all, against the law. It's stupid, but that's the way it is. That is why I waste my time in this country, trying to get contracts that justify my stays here. That is why my love is limited to passing children from the street.

- You pick up children on the street and you bring them here under the nose of the receptionist?

- For somebody who's making an investigation you are really very naive! There are hundreds of kids living on the streets of Bangkok. The meeting place is Robinson's, do you know where it is? That department store on the corner of Silom Road that's open till midnight.

Of course I know it. I nod my head rapidly. He goes on:

- All you have to do is sit on a bench opposite the store window and wait for a child to offer you his services. I get a room in a hotel in that part of town, the Rose for example, and for less than three hundred francs, I fuck a kid. The guys at the reception desk never ask questions, the police are down at the corner and the child really loves these two or three hours of love. Where do you see it's against the law? It isn't. In other places, it's not so easy to do what I do.

- Other places?

- I know Sri Lanka well. When people like me abandoned the Philippines because it got too dirty, too ugly, and more than anything else, too sad, the guidebooks sang the praises of the hotel facilities in Colombo. Now, ten years later, the authorities of Sri Lanka are still fighting to stop these encounters. Without much success. Why? Because the kids love it as much as we do. I can't see any other explanation.

- There isn't any "new love," only children who live on the streets, who need a few dollars, sometimes a little affection, and who often don't have any other choice than to go with people like you. Give them a roof, food and a school and you'll see if they still love "it" so much!

- Bah! I'm going back to Saigon in a few days. At night, on Catinat Street, kids from six to twelve offer their services. For ten dollars, they do absolutely everything. And for ten dollars more, the hotel keepers close their eyes. All you have to do is pick these kids up. They could beg for a living, but what they want is love. And that is what I need to give. So... you don't have to look any farther; Asiatic children are born lovers, with a sexuality that comes out of their pores. They love getting love from adults just as much as we love their infantile bodies.

Now Alain has gone back to his civilized language, his "cultural" monologue, that roundabout way of speaking that he can keep up for hours, far from crude reality but so close to the virtual world he has invented piece by piece. I have heard these arguments hundreds of times from other people who were, perhaps, less brilliant, less refined than he is but who talk about the same thing. I don't want to let him get carried away with his delirium. I interrupt him, go back to reality:

- Alain, when the gym teacher sexually abused you when you were eleven, he did it in the name of "new love," too. Remember, he hurt you very much physically. You suffered psychologically for twenty-five years after that. Since then, shut away in your secret, you, too, rape children in your own way. And you do it to make your suffering bearable. To accept the unacceptable: what you had to bear as a child. To forget that no adult came to your aid and that they betrayed you. The "new love" you talk about is based on the years of sexual abuse that you had to bear in total silence, on your own trauma!

Silence. I have gone too far. Too bad. No, better that way. I tried. Alain has regained his self control; he stands up, folds his napkin and gives me a forced but polite smile:

- Please excuse me for a moment. I must go to the men's room. Do you mind waiting here for me?

When he leaves the terrace, I know he will not be back.

I wait a good twenty minutes, my coffee gets cold. It is after one in the morning. I ask for the bill but the waiter answers that "The gentleman has already paid it." I cross the deserted lobby of the Oriental Hotel. I am not angry, just very sad and filled with compassion for this child who was sexually abused and who has become a distressed adult. Poor "crocodile"!

14.

JOHN, FRIEND, BROTHER...
TRAITOR

Monday morning, my watch says it is six o'clock. Already! I have the impression that I haven't slept at all. Last night, listening to Alain, I came to understand that behind the monstrosity of pedophilia, we find first of all a distressed adult, a former kid who also was raped by an adult pedophile. This observation requires a wider analysis of the problem. Why is it that no specialized service in Europe is taking care of these child abusers? We speak about the Convention for Children's Rights, we organize colloquiums, and yet we do not follow up on these men condemned for abuse of minors. We give up by refusing hospital-prisons, by refusing to accept our responsibility in this sex tourism and by denying help to preventive facilities. Why?

We have completed eighty dossiers. We have verified the information given in three international guidebooks, met little children who are kept locked up and met "crocodiles" at the Suriwongse and in other hotels in the quarter. The guidebooks are not wrong: the YC, or Young Company of Spartacus, is only a front for little slaves. Local newspapers inform tourists about the range of sexual facilities, about how to obtain a virgin, prostitutes of all kinds, transvestites, little Chinese girls and little ten-year-old boys. A parallel commerce also exists for Thai men, who seem to frequent brothels for adult women just as the British frequent tearooms.

There is only one difference: the Thai don't go to bars where there are showgirls; they go to brothels where they choose a girl in less than three minutes and are finished with her in a quarter of an hour. Foreigners seem to appreciate bars such as the Pink Panther, where girls use their sex to uncap Coke bottles or "smoke" blond cigarettes in the same way, with their legs spread wide in front of a male audience that claps its hands in encouragement.

I do not want to judge adult prostitution; it has existed for centuries. To tell the truth, I really don't care! Narrow-minded moralists that scream at the least little *faux pas* society makes annoy me. Conquering Puritanism often conceals an illness of its preachers dressed in their Sunday best with a collar that is too stiff. I do not have the calling of a religious person. Why does everything always have to be mixed together? Adult prostitution on the streets of Europe's capitals and child slavery cannot be lightly put on the same plane. It seems that some people don't sees the difference. Howerver, the law and the courts drew a dividing line a long time ago between adult prostitution and those who answer "sexual liberty" when you speak to them of "kidnapping, illegal confinement and severe child abuse." But then again, pedophiles are past masters in the art of controversy. For us, the objective remains to demonstrate that they murder street children: they rape them, starve them, burn them with cigarettes, injure them with belt beatings, cut them with knives; the children are tortured because they do not want so-called "new love." And in the end they die from this abuse or from AIDS. Hey, fellow Anglo-Saxons! You worry about the ravages of AIDS in your circle of friends, you spend millions on research, you demand condoms in schools so your children won't be transformed into walking dead... and yet you close your eyes when your neighbor across the hall carries death to kids. As if, before going to a seedy hotel in Patpong, our "crocodiles" in coat and tie have never gone to the locker room at the local swimming pool. Don't tell me that they don't fiddle with these kids under the pretext that the other kids have slanted eyes. You like facts? Those are the facts.

We collected excellent information here. Not suppositions, but the children's own words and the words of those who abuse them. It is their words that are taped on our cassettes. We have no names or addresses that would allow us to arrest them. Once again, we are not police. And the monster behind this factory is too big for us. We will have to start working with the children as soon as possible to create our own network of intervention and information. For almost three weeks now we have been swimming in the turbulent waters of child prostitution. Now we must find the financial support we need. I will go back to Europe and start making the rounds once again of humanitarian organizations in France, Belgium, England... anywhere it may be necessary. I am going to lose Toy. There are only a few more days until the moment when a train at Kualong-pong will brutally separate us. He will not change his mind, it is useless to ask him again. When Toy became involved in this investigation he clearly stated his limits, and he superbly fulfilled his moral agreement without the least weakness.

We are at John's apartment for one last evening. Surprise. A suitcase is sitting on the rattan couch. His plaid shaving kit is in the bathroom. John is in Bangkok. This calls for a big bowl of fish soup and a bottle of white wine to celebrate our unexpected reunion. A quick shower and to work in the kitchen. The table is set and the candles are lit to the music of Mozart. I hope he will come home for dinner.

The door opens and John's athletic body fills the entrance; 6 foot 5, he looks like an American basketball player. We fall into each other's arms. What a joy to see each other this evening just a few hours before our departure! John has just come back from China, an official trip for some international organization. Under a program for medical and social cooperation with pediatric hospitals, he was able to visit hospital facilities for handicapped children.

He describes in detail these catastrophic institutions as parking places for children similar to those in most communist regimes. It is urgent that the Convention for Children's Rights, under the auspices of the United Nations, come into being. Time is flying. John's Swiss cuckoo clock in the kitchen strikes twelve. Already!

We give John the details of the latest stages of our investigation: children kept prisoners in the brothels, the vacation center in Pattaya for retired people, the dinner with Alain at the Oriental Hotel. For a long while he remains silent. Then, aggressively, he accuses us of preaching morals. We listen dumbfounded. Toy gets up and leaves the room without a word. I go over our arguments again, point by point, talk about how old Sonta is, tell him Sowit's story and about her mutilated hand and about kids abandoned on the street at dawn. I want to shake him:

- What I am telling you has nothing to do with strait-laced morals. They are facts!

John is stuck:

- I won't have anything to do with bars for adult whores or shows for homosexuals when the people are free! The culture here is different.

- John, stop speaking foolishness! That's not the question. Culture or no culture, we're talking about children, not adults. Child slavery is a crime! The Convention for Children's Rights is for Thai children, too, and not only for our dear little blonds, isn't it?

All at once, I have raised my voice. But John continues to speak about Asiatic culture and uses such poor arguments that even the most worthless ethnologist would turn pale. Now I am angry. My voice gets louder:

- John, imagine for a moment that it is your child, your little daughter that is locked up in a brothel, victim of pedophiles. Open your eyes, damn it! Look at the reality of this country. No culture can justify child slavery!

John doesn't answer. He goes to the bar, opens a bottle of whisky and pours himself a big glass.

We have worked in the camps together, defended the same causes, made an uproar with the Thai authorities when they went too far in their non-respect of human rights. I feel let down, immensely deceived. For several minutes I look at him silently. John stretches out his arms to me. I can't. I leave the room without looking at him.

Toy is lying on the bed in the bedroom. I kiss him tenderly on the forehead and he opens an eye:

- Don't be discouraged, little sister, you'll get it sooner or later.

I have a very bad night. I remember a conversation with Virginia, my colleague in the camp at Phanat-Nikom. She didn't like John; she said that his "interest" in the projects for street children was unhealthy, that without a doubt, he loved the children a little too much. We argued about this many times because I felt that she was wrong. And last night he told me that, above all, the street children are free! That foreigners take them to a room just to give them some place to sleep. That even he had rendered this kind of service in Bangkok and elsewhere. Strange. Now I doubt everything.

Toy left the apartment at dawn leaving a message scribbled on a piece of paper:

- Mally, you are wrong about John. Rendezvous at noon at Camely's Restaurant. Love. Toy.

At breakfast John is ill at ease. Referring to our dispute in a confused way, he says he had too much to drink and that also being tired, he had said any old thing. I tell him it doesn't matter and that I don't want to talk about it any more. We say goodbye at the entrance. He gives me a set of keys in case I should come back in the next few months. I barely thank him. Sitting in a taxi on my way to the city, I am overcome with sadness. Should I add this conversation to the long list of ambiguous conversations included in my report? No, being in doubt, I prefer to forget it.

Patpong: as usual before every departure, Toy is not very talkative. My train is at three o'clock and the plane for Brussels leaves at ten thirty p.m. We have decided to say goodbye on the sidewalk without any show of our feelings, as if we were going to see each other again that evening. Teelapon will continue to be our contact.

I have no address where I can send Toy a letter, no phone number I can call if I feel discouraged. I feel like a tight-rope walker in an empty circus tent without any safety net. If I fall, there won't be anyone to help me bandage my wounds. But a little voice tells me that I am not going to fall. It is two o'clock, the streets are jammed with people, the traffic is completely blocked on Silom Road. Toy is standing there among office employees and tourists.

Without saying goodbye, he touches his finger to his lips and gets into a taxi. The light turns green and the taxi disappears. Even though I am surrounded by crowds of people, I feel terribly alone. I walk toward the grand temple of Wat-Prakeo. Among the statues of Buddha and the monks dressed in orange, in this magic calm, I ask myself if my friend Toy finds his strength in a Buddhist education. Or if he is simply an exceptional man in this business that is tearing me apart?

The dining room of the Camely Restaurant where I go to pick up my bags is empty and the waiters are setting the tables for the evening. At four o'clock I am already on my way to the airport. No risk of being late! But the memory of how I was attacked all at once fills me with a fear I haven't felt in a long time. I would have liked to see my friends, Teelapon the Attorney and Païthoon the Prof, before leaving, but they are away in the north. At the airport, tourists are standing in line at the ticket counter. A Lufthansa flight is checking baggage. There are twenty-eight people in the first line, eighteen of them are unaccompanied men in tourist class. In the second line, there are thirty-four tourists, twenty-seven are men alone. As for the business class, seven people are standing in line, four of them are well-dressed dynamic looking executives. I could use the waiting time to count the number of unaccompanied men, but what for? The picture is quite clear. A little later, a flight for Tokyo is announced. There, too, the lines are mostly men alone who look like new company officers. Not one couple, not one woman in lines 1 and 2. The interest the Japanese have for prostitutes is well-known in Bangkok. Important companies in Tokyo offer a few days in Bangkok to the most high-performing executives. The trip includes airline ticket, hotel and one or two prostitutes for the duration of the stay. Patpong has an annexed street that we call Patpong 2, reserved for the Japanese. The clubs there are private; no white person or Thai can enter if they are not members. It is a closed network and reserved for these stange businessmen.

Some adult prostitutes described these Japanese consumers to us as being violent mechanical men who do not hesitate to brutalize women, whom they consider as objects. That is what they pay for! Young women in Patpong told us they categorically refuse Japanese clients. But they don't always have the choice. I remember Sowit and her story with the Japanese journalist.

In the waiting room, the flight Bangkok-Brussels is posted on the board.

Immediate boarding.

15.

BRUSSELS:
THE RACE FOR A SUBSIDY

As usual, it is raining in Brussels. No one knew the day of my arrival, so no one has come to meet me.

I am going to stay at the home of an English friend who is away working in Latin America for a few months. The apartment is huge: sixteen hundred square feet of floor space, empty rooms where he has put some objects collected from around the world, forgotten plants that have died. But best of all a comfortable bedroom with a Japanese bed of impressive dimensions. There is a large desk, a computer, a portable photocopying machine, a printer and a telephone. I could not have asked for more. I prepare a teapot of English tea and snuggle under the quilt.

I have a list of about fifty organizations in Europe that might likely be interested in accepting a program in favor of children. The slogan of *Médecins sans Frontières* comes back to me: "To be where others are not." I have seen their poster in infirmaries in Hong Kong, Thailand, Cambodia and China. This may be the first lead.

The sun is high as I reread my notes and arrange my documents in precise order. I have been at the computer for two days without once going out. The document is ready. I seal the envelopes, glue on the stamps and mail everything. In a few days I will call every organization and ask for an appointment with the project director.

Médecins du Monde could back the idea if the EEC would just agree to finance it. Philippe Laurent, founding member of *Médecins sans Frontières-Belgium*, is now in charge of *Médecins du Monde*. He suggests that we meet with our future Thai partners. We should leave next month. This decision should make me very happy, but that is not the case because *Médecins du Monde* in Brussels has limited means for its operations. I ask myself if we are not moving too fast, if such a visit is not going to give hopes that we will not be able to fulfill afterward. Furthermore, the President of *Médecins du Monde* in Paris has already contacted a production agency to send a cameraman with us. I don't like this attitude at all, but the machinery has already been put into motion and for the moment it is my only hope since I have not had any other replies to my letters. One organization promised to send my report to the EEC and support it. Later, much later, I will learn that the project was forgotten in the bottom of a drawer in Paris. As the months pass, I go from one office to another in Brussels, Paris and Beirut.

It is an interesting experience to learn the labyrinths of this kind of association, the fights for power and the intrigues that are never mentioned, the bouts of yelling and the heartbreak. Time passes but none of the organizations I speak with accept my project. Their excuses are many and simple: the budget is too large and it covers a three-year period, safety conditions are too precarious, the project is intended to help only a hundred children and there are no specialists in this field. Worse, the people I speak with doubt the responsibility of the people involved and wonder about my motives. Am I really a militant for children's rights or a kind soul who is a little too naive? All I have to offer are my convictions, my stature and my report. Only the head of *Médecins sans Frontières-France* explains, during a friendly but argumentative meeting, his reasons for refusing. Other Directors in London, Amsterdam and Paris promise to meet me or leave it said that they are out. I have the impression that the phantom of the West's responsibility makes them avoid me. This be bad for white man, Bwana...

Summer is already at the door. Attorney Teelapon telephones me often. I am a little discouraged, but I am still convinced that we are going to find the money. And we will prove to the skeptics that they were wrong.

In the meantime, *Médecins du Monde* asks me to accept the responsibility for a group of children of all nationalities between the ages of ten and sixteen who are going to spend two months on a sailing ship. This is a media project in which the children will be the ambassadors of their rights. The children are all from different countries: Pham, a little boy, ex boat-person from Vietnam; Guerson, a boy from Guatemala; Piotr from Poland; Hein from Cambodia, and so on. Stopovers are planned at Dakar in Senegal, Fort-de-France in Martinique and, last of all, the Statue of Liberty. The purpose of this long voyage is, in fact, to meet the Secretary General of the United Nations, Perez De Cuellar, in New York. The journey will last almost two months and during that time the children will participate in workshops to discuss the Charter for Children's Rights. For Magali, who lives in the suburbs of Paris, Mamadou, a child from Dakar, or Sami, a Lebanese in exile, the concepts are obviously different. There will be violent confrontations between the rich and the poor, bitter tears, hysterical laughter and, despite chaotic organization, sick children, an insufficient teaching staff and a very limited budget, an extraordinary amount of reflection. From Fort-de-France, the ship will continue without the children because of very bad weather conditions and because they are exhausted after many weeks at sea with hardly any wind.

New York, journey's end. We are glad to finish this mission. For four days, the fifteen kids want to do and see everything in this infernal city. These children are tremendous. This adventure was partially financed by the François-Xavier Bagnoud Association, a Swiss organization named for the helicopter pilot killed with Thierry Sabine during the Paris-Dakar race. The T-shirts of the two organizations, François-Xavier Bagnoud and *Médecins du Monde*, were forgotten in Paris by one of the organizers. What a disaster! In twelve hours we are supposed to meet with Perez De Cuellar. The children still have their old T-shirts from the first day but they are in deplorable condition. On the other hand, we have a supply of clothes bearing the initials of *Médecins du Monde*. In order to avoid conflict, the only solution is to find an automatic laundry in the area, wash, dry, iron and, most important, mend the holes in the old shirts. I spend the night taking care of this, and in the morning I proudly distribute the T-shirts to my fifteen little monsters.

In a good hotel, all the Directors and the "bigwigs" from Paris prepare for the meeting with the big man. Each child goes over what he is going to say and what he is going to ask in the name of his country and the children of the world: the right to an International Convention of Children's Rights. At the United Nations, security is on the alert. Every route has been checked and controlled.

When Hieng, a little Cambodian girl, sees the flag of what was once her country fluttering in the breeze, she breaks down in tears. Her state is now represented by the Khmer Rouge of Cambodia, the people who killed her family. Sami has a vision of a united Lebanon; the boy from Israel takes Amir, a ten-year-old boy from Palestine, by the hand. Today, children are the only real hope for a world without hate. Now as they read their recommendations one after the other, each in his own language, Perez De Cuellar listens to every message, moved by their conviction.

Standing behind the children for the official photo, the adults distinguish themselves by pushing each other to be sure to appear in the picture. The Directors from headquarters, whom we haven't seen since our departure, are there with a triumphant air. Once back in Europe, I learn that *Médecins du Monde* doesn't know what to decide about Thailand. I leave with my project under my arm and with the feeling of having participated in a big summer camp and having lost a lot of time.

During these last months, I met the Countess Albina du Bois Rouvray two or three times. A woman of about fifty whom everyone calls Albina, she has that dynamic drive of new business women. She is the Director of the François-Xavier Bagnoud Association, which financed a part of the children's voyage to New York. We talk about the prostitution and slavery of children in Thailand. She is shocked by the contents of our investigation-evaluation, and with the agreement of her Board of Directors, the François-Xavier Bagnoud Association offers us fifty percent of the budget needed for our project. This is a very generous offer, the first one that lets us begin to hope. The only requirement is that the children's home bear the name of François-Xavier Bagnoud. When her son, François-Xavier, died, Albina suffered grave depression for two years. Then she decided to create her own association in Switzerland. Its objective is to fight against the violations of children's rights. The Association now has offices in Geneva, Paris and New York. Since 1991 its actions in India, Kenya and the United States are centered on the problem of AIDS. Albina would have liked, furthermore, for the CPCR to create centers for children that are HIV positive. In the future, she will come to visit us two or three times a year in Bangkok and without fail at Christmas time. Since her son's death, Albina says she cannot stand the holiday season. The François-Xavier Bagnoud Association will finance half the budget of our project for three years and we will send them a monthly report; *Médecins sans Frontières* will guarantee follow-up of the project, take care of the technical aspects and control activity finances. But we are not there yet! For now, we still have to find the other fifty percent.

The months pass. One night in Brussels I cannot sleep so I go to a night library. Behind a shelf, I run into one of the Directors of *Médecins sans Frontières-Belgium*. We talk a few minutes about our projects and of course about Thailand. He is convinced that *Médecins sans Frontières* will accept the project. In his opinion, the idea of working with a local Thai partner seems to be a "plus" for the dynamics of the association in Brussels. One week later, after many meetings, the Board of Directors gives its agreement. We still have to finalize the conditions of partnership between the François-Xavier Bagnoud Association, *Médecins sans Frontières* and the European Economic Community, which has decided to support the project. In the end, the budget will be shared as follows: fifty percent by François-Xavier Bagnoud, forty percent by the EEC and the remaining ten percent by *Médecins sans Frontières*.

I remember this meeting on the first floor of the EEC building very well. I never thought I would have to go to Bangkok to personally get the wheels rolling, but that is one of the conditions stipulated by the financial backers: be personally on the spot as "coordinator." This decision makes me very happy, but at the same time, it fills me with fear. Will I be able to stand the reality of Bangkok's streets every day? Will I be able to live with this gut fear? Jean-Paul is far away. How will he take to this separation? We meet in Champagne, France for a few days. He accepts the idea that I will be exposed to danger again and finds a compromise: he is going to look for a job in Asia so we can see each other often and perhaps live together. I can hardly believe that a man would turn his career upside down for me. Between my break-up with Philippe and what I saw of men in Bangkok, I thought I had lost faith in men. With Jean-Paul, everything is so simple.

After listening to the tape recordings and seeing the pictures of the children in the brothels, Jean-Paul encourages me every step of the way. For the time being, he has to go back to Africa. I won't be leaving for six weeks. What can I do in the meantime? The European Community is looking for experts to carry out an investigation in Roumania regarding children that cannot be recuperated. Rumania? Why not?

16.

RUMANIA: THE DEATH HOUSES
FOR THE CHILDREN OF MOLDAVIA

We are six specialists. With a stimulation test and a questiomnaire, we are to visit the provinces of Roumania and examine about fifteen children every day, orphans from one to fifteen who have been selected as a sample. The directors of these institutions see our visits as an inspection and, in some cases, think charges will be brought against them. They need heaters, toys and powdered milk, not information on the condition of their charges. I clearly remember one appalling visit in Moldavia...

We have been driving on a country road for two hours. The district's head social assistant accompanying me is a cold, austere woman, no doubt a member of the Party. The car turns off to the right and continues on a dirt road through a dense forest. It takes at least another ten minutes to reach the orphanage. What is an institution for handicapped children doing way out here in the woods?

What am I going to find behind the thick gray walls of this building? At the entrance, a man dressed in gray is sweeping the court. In the hall, a putrid smell makes me feel sick to my stomach, and adults and children can be heard screaming. A nurse takes me to the doctor's office. Gesticulating children behind glass doors seem like little imprisoned animals. They all wear shirts of the same gray cloth or are running around naked. This is not the first institution I have visited, but this one looks like something right out of a nightmare.

The male nurse explains in unsure French the workings of this establishment, which houses two hundred children who have been classified as "irredeemable" by a commission of Roumanian specialists. I ask for a doctor but there isn't any and hasn't been for two years. The last doctor to come here for a training period stayed for less than a week before packing his suitcases and leaving without a word. There was no replacement after that.

I ask about treatment for the sick children and discover that Mircea, the male nurse explaining things to me, is... a patient in this institute. He came here at the age of ten because of an irreversible physical handicap. The young man has difficulty walking because both his feet are deformed. His intellectual development seems normal. He writes, reads correctly and manages the pharmacy like a good storekeeper. He shows me the box of syringes and mimics sessions for shots. Some years ago, an old doctor who directed the institute taught him the rudiments of medicine. After the doctor died, Mircea took his place. He treats colds, gives shots of vitamins and calms attacks of epilepsy. And he breathes a little ether when the children's screams keep him from sleeping. There is a woman in charge of the institute, but she has gone to town to look for a doctor; a child on the first floor is sick. It is time to begin the test. In the big register for admissions, I find the names of two hundred and eleven children. I point to fifteen names. Mircea looks for their numbered files. The office is in a state of indescribable chaos! It is impossible to find files 3 and 176; as for 45, 66 and 123, they died in the last year.

The first child comes into the room carried by an attendant wearing a gray apron and rubber slippers. Bogdan is a ten-year-old boy who looks no more than five or six. His body is wrapped in rags stinking from urine. I take off every layer and try to smile at him. His little legs are mall-formed and bent up over his abdomen. There are huge sores on his skinny knees. A green liquid has dried on his skin. First of all, a bath! Mircea demonstrates that he is quite competent and quickly brings a metal basin, a dingy towel and a bar of soap, which comes from Germany.

The child plays in his bath and seems to be really happy, a rare feeling! Sitting on the rusty table covered with a threadbare sheet for the occasion, he lets me treat him without a cry! He plays with a ball and other educational toys I have brought. He listens, understands and can repeat every exercise without one single mistake.

If he doesn't know how to read or write, it's because, once classified irredeemable, no school here will teach him. Irredeemable!

If he had a wheelchair, this child could participate in normal activities and probably overcome his retardation. There are only two pages in his file to cover ten years of his life: abandoned at one month, a period of time in an orphanage, then sent to a center for irredeemable children because of his handicap. This boy has a physical malformation and they have condemned him for it. In the hallway, attendants are arguing in loud voices. I question my assistant nurse again. In a whisper, he makes me understand that the reason for this commotion can be found on the first floor. I certainly want to see this case that has the personnel so agitated. I rush up the stairs and down the hall where I find dark little rooms where bunches of children hang despairingly over the railings of their beds. The mattresses are soaked with urine and every room stinks.

At the end of the hall, the attendants have started arguing again.

I approach them and see that they are arguing about a child in a small bed in room No. 9. Its body is already rigid and almost black. It has been dead several hours, the large eyes open, lying in a soaked diaper. At the end of the room, four beds are stuck against the wall. A dozen children are crying and hanging over the metal barriers. No one has thought to take these babies away from this sad sight. Anger fills me. In a cold voice I demand that the children be immediately taken to another section. The Department's social assistant that accompanied me says stiffly:

- This is not your business. Your mission is on the ground floor. We will take care of this ourselves.

Too much is too much. I am not going to wait for some so-called doctor to arrive before doing something. Two things are evident. One, a child has been dead for quite some time; two, children are in anguish and urgently need help. I move the beds and push these cages of children toward the hallway with all my strength. A young attendant takes the beds to another room. I can see tears running down her cheeks. At the end of the hall, the chief attendant motions in anger. I throw him a scornful look knowing at the same time that I will pay for humiliating him this way. But I don't care.

My eyes meet those of the young attendant. She is leaning on the banister. I motion for her to come with me into the room of the tragedy. She hesitates a moment before joining me. The skeletal little body on the bed is that of a girl not yet a year old. A green undershirt with little chicks covers the body. Its little members are covered with brownish spots, the skin discolored in some places. Was the child HIV positive? It could be. Without a doubt, it was a victim of malnutrition and dehydration. In this place where the children are considered irredeemable, the least I can do is wash the body and wrap it in a clean cloth. The attendants keep coming in and out of the room making me feel like an actress in a very bad play: a crazy European woman risking who-knows-what contamination. One thing is sure: no one will shake my hand good-by when I leave. I cannot blame them. They are pure products of a totalitarian regime that has probably killed their last bit of feeling. By the end of the day I have examined ten children. More than half need to be transferred immediately to a different type of institute.

As night falls, I look around for the social assistant, but the car is no longer in the courtyard. The director arrives wrapped in a white smock. Everyone has left and there is no way for me to return to the city. So this is the price I have to pay for my insolence: spend the night here. For dinner, the two of us share a piece of fat pork and greasy potatoes. The tomato juice the cook offers me expired at least two years ago. Around ten p.m. we go upstairs to sleep. To my surprise, the director opens two folding beds in her office, the room where she has slept for the last ten years. She takes three tranquilizers from the bottle on the night table and swallows them quickly; enough to dose a horse. It is impossible for me to sleep, so I walk the halls. The children are alone, completely left to themselves. The smallest ones rock violently against the metallic sidings of their cribs, the bigger ones pull themselves out of their beds but then cannot find their way back in the dark. An attendant sleeps sitting on an old wooden chair. Winter, with its temperatures below zero, must be a nightmare here. With total indifference, the children are left to die of hunger or from the lack of care, but most of all, from the lack of love. Death walks the halls here. Lying on my camp bed that night, I don't close my eyes a single minute. The children's cries pierce the night like a last plea for help.

In the morning I make a round of the rooms. The children are sleeping soundly three or four to a bed, their eyes swollen from crying. Some lie staring blankly at the ceiling in a state of psychological death; these children have not cried for a long time.

Several weeks later I take the plane back to Brussels but the faces of hundreds of children haunt me for a long time.

I must admit it: I wouldn't have had the courage to work very long in this kind of institution. Fortunately, others did.

17.

RETURN TO BANGKOK: GETTING DOWN TO WORK!

Nothing has changed in Bangkok, the most detestable city I know. Traffic is as dense as ever, the pollution sticks to your skin and tourists roam the main streets dressed in shorts and grotesque hats. I decided not to tell my Thai friends when I would be arriving, so there is no one to meet me at the airport. I go to a small hotel on Sukhumvit Road. I want to have twenty-four hours to calmly realize that this is where I am going to live for at least one year. It is night in the city as I walk the small soi, reach Ploenchit Road and cross the bridge. I can see why beggars seem to be rare in this Asian capital: they live under the bridges.

Robinson's store is still open so I have time to buy a few things. As I leave, I stop a few moments on the steps of the main entrance. Robinson's, on the corner of Silom Road, has always been a meeting place for pedophiles and street children. A man about fifty is sitting on a bench. Beside him, a young boy around ten is eating an enormous hamburger. The adult's hand moves up and down the boy's thighs. The child pushes the man's caressing hand away many times. A little farther away, a foreigner, somewhere in his thirties, has come to pick up a child. His taxi, double-parked, waits for the deal to be made. A child under twelve leaves a group of kids and joins the foreigner at the edge of the sidewalk. The man and the child talk for a few minutes, a second child joins them, the man nods his head yes and the child gets into the taxi. No, nothing has changed in Bangkok.

I walk in the direction of my hotel. The night is mild and the sky is full of stars, street lamps light the avenue with many shops. I see a little girl sitting in a bush in Lumpini Park. What is she doing there all alone? She is wearing a short red dress, her long hair is all tangled, and she is

126

dragging a piece of cloth behind her. Even though it is almost ten p.m. and we are in a city of six million people, she is all alone.

I go up to her, smile and dig in my grocery bag for something to eat. I have just bought some sweet rice sticks wrapped in banana leaves. Suddenly she seems more like a wild cat than a little girl as she grabs the rice bars and gobbles them down. Her whole face becomes an impish smile. She rubs her mouth with the back of her hand. She follows me step for step for almost twenty minutes until she sees a gang of kids on the other sidewalk. My heart almost stops as I watch her cross the street. She dashes toward her friends without even looking. Squealing brakes, blasting horns and drivers' yells fill the air. On the other side, a dozen kids take off at a run. For this time, she made it.

Boys living on the street no doubt fare better than girls. The networks of prostitution soon catch little girls and lock them up in the brothels.

After a night's sleep, it is high time to contact Attorney Teelapon and "Prof" Pathoon. They pick me up an hour later and drive me to the Center for the Protection of Children's Rights where a room has been prepared for me; our adventure has begun. Teelapon gets busy on the telephone and arranges our first appointments for tomorrow morning.

We open an international bank account so funds can be transferred from Brussels. The language barrier becomes a problem. At every question, the bank employee answers: "OK, I know..." But she cannot tell us anything more. We're off to a good start. Luckily, there is Pathoon with his wonderful French. Ah! Pathoon and Teelapon. Teelapon is by far the most charming person I know. He has the charm of old France and the finesse of Asia. In his life, just as in his work, no detail is left to chance. For him, sleep is lost time. It is precious.

A small team works at the Center for the Protection of Children's Rights: social assistants, lawyers, teachers, educational specialists. In the evening, volunteer students from the university, nurses and doctors come to help. They man the telephone, go through piles of paper, sort hundreds of photos and put data into the computer. These ungratifying, basic daily tasks are all taken care of by volunteers ranging in age from twenty to sixty who have one point in common, one thing that brings them together: they all have rebellion burning in their eyes. How can it be otherwise in this country where the army has been controlling everything for so many years, where human rights are derided daily, where people are often thrown into death-house prisons only for political reasons, and where corruption is rampant. Where the commerce of sex has reached appalling dimensions.

The Center for the Protection of Children's Rights, called CPCR, was founded in 1984. This project was implemented by Teelapon and the present director, Sanphasit. The courageous goal of the CPCR is to register all forms of exploitation of children. The team verifies every piece of information, tries to track down situations of slavery. They clandestinely work their way into the network of child prostitution, a job of persistence that bears fruit: every year, children are freed. But the team is wearing itself out for lack of support and financial means. Our first objective is to make the CPCR a veritable center of operations. Personnel must be hired, the office reorganized and money spent for materials. So far, so good.

Next, a receiving center must be opened for the young victims of prostitution. For the moment, children rescued are living in the office until a solution is found. This can take as little as a few days or, perhaps, several months.

Many children arrive in a state of shock; others need treatment for their injuries. They cannot all be treated in the same way. We need more privacy. This is the most urgent problem to solve. For several weeks, we search for a house that is spacious yet offers privacy. We would like to have a big yard where the children can play. To assure their security, we must find a house that is far away from the hot quarters of downtown. The problem is that owners do not trust tenants like us. They are afraid the building will be ruined and, above all, they fear reprisal by the Mafia.

But we finally find our house less than ten minutes away from the CPCR! This beautiful villa is near the river on a very narrow residential *soï* where the speed limit is fifteen miles per hour. As soon as it is furnished, the home will be able to receive a good twenty children. To improve security, we have a brick wall built all around the yard, install a strong iron gate at the entrance, hire two night watchmen and arrange for special surveillance from private security guards in the area. But none of this will daunt our adversaries of the Mafia.

It is time to give the house a coat of paint. Dressed in work clothes, about ten of us set to work painting, collecting rubbish and cleaning the garden, but there is always someone who stops me from touching a paint brush or a broom. Teelapon laughs as he watches me look for a job. I begin to get impatient. Do I look so funny with a rag in my hand? A few more little things to do and the house will be perfect. We go shopping from store to store, comparing prices and buying furniture. The house is finally ready and waiting for the first children.

Four teachers will take care of the children, two professors from the School of Fine Arts will teach painting on silk, two teachers will come every evening to give reading lessons, and an old music professor has promised to organize lessons in the garden. Our nurse, Mrs. Daeng, will care for the children's ills and listen to their problems. Three times a week we will take the children to the swimming pool where a volunteer gym teacher will organize games and relaxation. As for religion, only the children who want to will be taken to the Buddhist temple near here. In a corner of the garden, we have already prepared the traditional "Soul House", a sort of altar where the children can lay fruit and rice, offerings that are supposed to keep the evil spirits away from the house. A neighboring Thai family has given us a pretty red and blue swing. Everyone loves this swing, even the sixteen-year-old girls, the oldest in the home! But we absolutely do not want to turn this house into a first class hotel, and, therefore, every child will have a chore to do in the home.

Every Monday a chart will be posted showing the job and responsibility of each child and teacher. Meals will be eaten in the garden on round tables: special moments of great joy and great sadness. I love to spend my nights at the home. Nighttime always leads to the confiding of secrets and intimate talks with one of the children. We will often sleep on the terrace protected by a big mosquito net, and during the night I will hear the girls struggle against the nightmares of their recent past. Yes, the night, when the fears masked during the day come to life. It is a time of crying out and tears; a time of jumping up and going to reassure the children, comfort them with the air of a seemingly self-assured professional.

Everything is finally ready. I count the days. I know that a rescue action is planned for this Wednesday. Poo, a young teacher in charge of detection, has finished an investigation. He has discovered a brothel on the edge of town where about fifteen women and children are kept prisoners. The manager, a Thai, has already had some problems with the police. His first bar was closed because he didn't pay the bribes demanded by the intermediaries. The consumers are Thai and, on rare occasions, a foreigner, most probably expatriates. The place is really too far away from the center of town for the tourists. Pretending to be a client, Poo the investigator was able to meet two little girls. They come from the north and speak Thai very poorly. We have asked Yake, the chief of a village in the mountains, to join us. Yake the rebel is that extraordinary man who is fighting against the kidnapping of children in his region. I spent a few days in his village with his wives with the gold teeth. He knows the dialect very well and his contact with the children is excellent.

Moo, a social assistant, is working untiringly to track down children locked in a factory assembly line. He has questioned people in the area and spent hours closely watching the comings and goings around the building. The case is a delicate one and as much information as possible must be collected before asking the police to intervene. So often here, this kind of case is filed away without anything being done, especially if members of the government or important public figures are implicated. Traffic in children represents an important source of revenue for the numerous intermediaries. Not hundreds, but millions of bahts are involved. According to our information, about twenty little boys are locked up in this factory. They work fifteen hours a day and sometimes are beaten. We were tipped off by a licensed worker, who decided to talk for revenge.

I would like to accompany Poo and Moo, the men on the spot, when the children will be freed, but Teelapon is inflexible: first of all, I must be familiar with every phase of their work. Freeing the children often gives rise to a series of problems: the violent reaction of the brothel keepers, conflict with corrupted police, and, above all, revenge by the Mafia, which does not like our interference. Every liberation means a considerable loss of money for their network. Teelapon feels that a European is all too easy to recognize and he has made it a point of honor to guarantee my safety. It is well known that I have been sleeping at the CPCR, but it is becoming more and more unsafe to go on staying here. I have the impression of working in this cramped building twenty hours out of twenty-four. Since I plan to live in Bangkok for at least one year, it is time for me to find an apartment. Sanphasit, the Director, and Attorney Teelapon have reservations about my project. They are worried about my safety. We reach a compromise. I will find lodging in a relatively safe quarter, like the one where the CPCR is located, such as Saint-Louis or Swanploo. We find a small, two-storey Chinese house in a *soï* parallel to Pathoon's. The Chinese family is looking for a new tenant since the previous one was sent to prison - five years for drug dealing. The house is small but quite nice. The only negative point is that the front door, facing the street, is an iron lattice grill and everyone can see me day and night. I think I will soon become the main attraction on this little street. So what! I will only be home at night. The rent is low, Pathoon lives less than five minutes away, and there is even a telephone. The agreement is made and a few days later I move into my new home.

I avoid the kitchen, which is overrun by rats. I prefer to buy my meals on the street from peddlers or accept small meals from Mrs. Pathoon. My neighbors get up before sunrise and from five o'clock in the morning my room smells of fried fish.

Often, with Pathoon the Prof, I take bus No. 49, which is usually packed with people. Elegant women, wearing nylon pantyhose even when it's hot, and men in shirts and ties are stuck to each other. When we get off twenty minutes later, I feel completely rumpled, but my colleague's shirt appears perfectly intact. At the office, the team laughs when they see my disheveled air and it takes me some time in the restroom on the first floor to regain a normal appearance. Sometimes I stay at the CPCR to sleep when it is very late at night or when I am discouraged by the idea of returning home alone.

Coming into the office this morning, I can see that they have worked all night. The main room is black with smoke and coffee cups are scattered everywhere. Teelapon is already on the telephone and children are sitting on mats on the first floor mezzanine. I sit down across from Teelapon. He looks so tired; his eyes are red from staying up all night and chain-smoking as usual. He points to the children. A battle has been won!

After putting the phone down, he takes me to the children. Nine little girls are sitting pressed to one another. Their faces are swollen from crying and some show clear signs of abuse: cigarette burns and badly healed sores. Unconsciously, I touch my shoulder. The memory of those round scars will be impressed in my mind forever.

The girls are between ten and fourteen years old. Twelve adult women found in the same brothel were sent to a refuge for abused women. But three young women from Burma were taken to the immigration prison. Oh! I am already familiar with the corruption, violence and maltreatment of this dreadful place.

Attorney Teelapon is also familiar with this prison. He knows that the three women will have to be visited regularly in order to protect them.

A recently employed psychologist questions the young girls. We must have as much information as possible about them to be able to look for their families and to write a complete report for the lawyer and the judge if we want to take the pimp to court.

Yake the rebel is also at the Center today. It took him many hours of walking and a twelve-hour bus ride to reach Bangkok. He speaks Thai fluently as well as many tribal languages. He is a fascinating person, a dark-skinned mountain dweller from the north with enormous hands, hands that have worked the earth a lot - and know how to hold a gun. Yake is married to three women and is planning to marry a fourth very soon. He takes the kidding well. We sit down together. I know he has news of Toy and Sonta. Teelapon has told me that he hasn't heard from Toy for several months, but I don't think he is telling me the truth. Through Pathoon, I question our friend Yake. When I ask him for news about Toy, his face becomes blank and he turns aside to speak to Pathoon.

O.K., I understand, they have a secret that I have no right to know. I respect their silence even if I find it unjust. I cannot resign myself to the fact that I will never see Toy again.

As for Sonta, the situation is not very bright. Everything went fine for the first few months, then she developed AIDS, and now she is constantly sick. Yake tells me she has a severe cough and bleeding abscesses in her mouth and on her lips. Her family is doing their best and taking care of the child as model parents. The village healers tried treating her with plants, roots and buffalo horn, but obviously without results.

There is no doubt about it... Sonta is going to die. My sadness is immense. Sitting at his desk, Teelapon has followed our conversation from behind his newspaper. He gets up, takes me to the kitchen and makes me take a drink of tea. We have always spoken plainly about our feelings regarding these fleeting victories followed by terrible defeat, about the lost battles against the illness of this century. As in every discussion, Teelapon finds the right words, words that are reassuring and, above all, that make you want to continue:

- Listen, Mally. Sonta was returned to her family; she became a child again even if it was only for a few months, even though we knew that this illness could only end in death. We gained a little time, Mally! A few months of happiness for this little ten-year-old girl. Do you think that comes free?

I lower my head.

- So? Look! Think of the months she would have had to spend in that brothel, and think of the months she lived up there, in the mountains. In her mountains! At home, with her parents, her brothers and sisters, where she can hug her mother. Her mother, Mally, not a German or French tourist. This happiness is priceless, you know. Death can take her, she was condemned anyway. But at least she won't end her life in a brothel in Patpong. And her mother will be holding her hand right up to the end.

I can't say anything, I just want to cry. Teelapon raises my head:

- Come on now, we have to take care of the children that have just arrived. They need you, too!

The next morning we begin our daily meeting with a report on the condition of the girls that were freed yesterday. There are twelve of us sitting around the big table listening to the report of this rescue. My friend Pathoon translates word for word the parts I do not understand. Upon request by the CPCR, the police arrived at the place of rendezvous on the corner of highway No. 4, north of the city. In the past there have been too many problems with certain police: escapes, abortive actions. After that, Teelapon decided to establish meeting places rather than give a precise address. The police do not like this technique, which they interpret, and rightly so, as a lack of confidence.

With a police car, the team of four went to the spot. Their raid was quick. The police entered with guns drawn, the managers were taken with hardly any resistance. Clients took advantage of the confusion to slip out. Moo said there were two foreigners at the bar. While the police controlled the personnel's identity, the team checked every room. Women were running everywhere and the children were in a state of shock. Panic. When everyone was reassembled in the main hall, Teelapon explained what was going to happen and order was re-established.

Identities were verified, pictures were taken, testimony was given to a police assistant and everyone was searched. Guns, knives and wooden clubs were found in a cupboard with a double bottom. The children were probably kidnapped in the northern part of the country. On an average, they have been in the brothel from eight to twelve months, having several customers a day. Of course all the girls show signs of having been beaten with clubs and burned with cigarettes. Some of them were raped collectively; others were sent to customers who are a little particular: they did not pay to go to bed with the girls but only to have the pleasure of beating them. According to the girls' testimony, the clients were Thai, Chinese from Hong Kong and a few Occidentals, always the same. One of these had rented a little girl for the week:

- The boss knows him well, says a woman. He trusted him.

At the hospital, the girls are given a complete medical examination including an HIV test to determine which are eventually HIV positive as well as a series of tests to detect sexually transmissible diseases. 'Detect' also means to explain the illness and its consequences to the child. This poses a problem to members of the team. The are not ready to face this matter yet. Of course it is easier not to say anything, but I refuse. It won't be easy with traumatized kids, often illiterate, a Thai society which speaks of AIDS only as a fatality and a team that does not like to face this kind of problem; it is going to be very difficult!

I have found an ally for this in Mrs. Daeng, the young nurse. She is a sensitive, calm woman in her thirties who talks about AIDS with perfect knowledge because she has taken care of patients in the final phases of this illness at the hospital where she worked. She knows that the Thai refuse the truth and that their awakening is going to be brutal. Mrs. Daeng is convinced that we are heading straight for catastrophe: millions of Thai will soon be HIV positive.

We must admit that when we think of the future, me included, we try to minimize the problem because working with children the majority of whom are HIV positive is one of the most difficult things in the world! I know from this experience that there is nothing more unacceptable than the death of a child.

At the CPCR, Moo, our man on the spot, has completed his investigation of a suspected workshop: now he is certain that children are kept locked up there. Teelapon has decided to intervene. The district's Police Chief is reluctant and wants to first check out the information himself. Teelapon and Moo decide to meet with the police officer. If the cop refuses, we will find a journalist to publish an article about the matter. That is enough to scare them a little. The team fights on all fronts at the same time.

The psychologist organizes the children's transfer to the new home we have baptized with the name François-Xavier Bagnoud. The Thai on our team are already calling it "Banoonrak" because the pronunciation of François-Xavier Bagnoud is too complicated for them. Four adults will live there with the children day and night. We, too, promise to do our share: at least a few hours of time and one meal per week to understand their problems and also so they will not be cut off from the rest of the team. I carefully respect the informal hierarchy established at the CPCR. I feel that I am here only to assist them in their project, not to implement mine. It's not easy. Sometimes I have to accept decisions that I don't like. And then I have to defend these decisions with the directors at the head office in Brussels.

The days turn quickly into weeks. After a while, Jean-Paul is sent to Hanoi. We will certainly see each other on week-ends. He continues to be enthusiastic, always ready to listen to me, to encourage me. He subscribes to numerous international magazines and prepares quite a dossier of articles on child slavery for me, sending me the latest publications from around the world, mainly Canada. All of this helps us to perfect our methods of action.

Two families have been found north of Chiang-Rai; perhaps the parents of the three little girls rescued from the brothel.

Yake, the tribal chief, is convinced that they are families whose children strangely disappeared six months earlier under strange circumstances. Their description corresponds to the three little girls. That very evening we pile into the all-terrain vehicle we have received and drive all night. Teelapon, Moo and Poo, the investigator, take turns at the wheel. It takes us ten hours to reach Metchai. There, we put on our backpacks and walk; I have learned to love walking! Teelapon, always so full of attention, carries my pack. Four hours later we reach the meeting place with Yake.

He is there waiting, a cloth sack on his shoulder and always the same proud, rebellious air of a mountain tribal chief. We continue our march on red soil under a cloudy sky and oppressive heat. We drink at village fountains while the village children stare at us. With a really good all-terrain vehicle, it seems as if it would be easy to come up here and snatch children who are off by themselves. Five more miles. My legs hurt and my shoes slip on the sandy road. I try to think about other things, my grandmother from whom I have just received a letter. Her eyesight is getting worse and her writing is almost illegible. I called her before leaving Bangkok. Her voice was warm, full of life. I don't suffer from not seeing her because I know that distance makes no difference in our relationship. And then there's Jean-Paul.

Up ahead we can see an enormous village, thatched roofs and smoke from wood ovens rising above the vegetation. An old man wearing a hat decorated with pieces of silver comes to meet us. His eyes fasten on me and his smile shows all his teeth. Yake translates what he says:

- This is the first time that a white woman has come to the village, he is pleased yet worried. He has never seen hair made of straw!

Yake makes fun of me and suggests that I leave the chief a few locks of hair as a souvenir. He laughs.

The sun is slowly going down the side of the mountain. The old chief's house is made of brown wood and thatch with a bamboo terrace overlooking the village. Fifteen people live in this house: Asok, the chief, his three wives and nine children. Smoking hot tea in bamboo goblets is served on a cane tray. The rules require that we share the evening meal before any discussions. The women are busy around the fire. Plates of meat and perfumed rice are placed on mats. The chief's son serves us an alcoholic beverage made from rice. I take just a sip to do honor to this glass of friendship. My mouth is on fire. Discreetly Moo motions to me and exchanges my glass with his, which is already empty. It is time now. Two families are waiting for a signal from the chief to climb the stairs and join us. Strangely, the two women must wait patiently at the bottom of the stairs. Only the men can participate in the meal. They do not speak Thai but the Akha language. Discussions proceed slowly at the pace of translation. The children of the two families disappeared six months ago this very day. Teelapon prefers to inform them immediately about the existence of a network of prostitution. If these are really their daughters, they will have to accept the horror of what happened to them. These people have no idea of what can happen in Bangkok. They live here in another world. Yake speaks to them at length about his experience, about our work at the CPCR and about what happens to the children in Bangkok.

Attorney Teelapon opens his pack, takes out copies of papers and pictures of each child. The men examine the pictures closely by the light from a kerosene lamp. The two fathers raise their heads, say a few words in Akha. Yake translates: these are their daughters, there is no doubt about it.

A young adolescent says he recognizes two other little girls from a neighboring village. Teelapon suggests sending Moo and Poo the investigator to verify this precious information tomorrow. Yake the rebel will take two men to Bangkok to pick up the little girls. This is an excellent opportunity to invite them to work with us. A member of our team will take the occasion to show them the capital and explain the risks to children here. Once back at the village, the chief will tell about what he saw. This method of action will prove to be very effective.

The sky is full of stars. I can see the shadows of the villagers as they drink alcohol and talk. The sound of the mountain radio station reaches me. My mind wanders as I sit leaning against the bamboo wall. I see Toy, Sonta, the villagers and that little hand waving behind us. I will never forget them.

In the morning Moo and Poo leave to verify the information concerning the nearby village. Paithoon will stay at Chiang-Rai to spread the description of other children and Teelapon and I will return to Bangkok with Yake and the men. Another raid is planned for tomorrow evening in the capital and I don't want to miss it.

We drive through the rice paddies. Here, there are no schools for children within less than three hours walking. There is no hope of emancipation for this population excluded from the country's economic development. Their harvest, bought at a low price by intermediaries from the city, allows the community to get along. Their is no doctor, no family planning, no hygiene. The farmers live with their bare feet in the earth, clinging to their mountains. The rich era of cultivating opium is over. Burned by the authorities, the poppy fields were planted with tea. Of course the opium plantations still exist. They have just migrated to the other side of the Burmese border a few miles from here. Now the men cross the jungle, work for a season, then come back to the village with a little money in their pockets.

18.

A NIGHT OF HORROR

We arrive at the CPCR at six o'clock in the morning. The police have called. By chance, some little girls have been freed from a brothel. A fire broke out in the kitchen of the building and the firemen rescued the children from the rubble. They are in a state of shock. I hurry to the home to alert the nurse, Mrs. Daeng; we must prepare a room for these children. The other children are still sleeping and the house is still quiet. The little girls from the burned brothel arrive. They are covered with soot, their clothes are in rags and they have superficial burns on their arms. These girls are Akas, originally from the north of Thailand. Fortunately there are other little girls here from the same region; the new girls will not feel too lonely in our home. They all have gonorrhea, a sexually transmissible disease that must be treated with massive doses of antibiotics. Worse, three of them are HIV positive. The girls are between ten and twelve years old. One of them, the youngest, already shows signs of the disease. Already! How unjust!

The team reacted very badly when they heard it. One teacher wanted the three children to be put in quarantine. Just what I was afraid of: fear, incomprehension, exclusion. We will have to talk with the teachers again. If we accept the least compromise, we'll be done for. If members of the team want to resign, let them; we will agree. But before that, we must prove to them that they can handle this problem by just taking the necessary precautionary measures.

Right now we have to take care of formalities with the police. An agent from the central office is waiting, sitting on the sofa in the lounge. These Thai cops definitely have the appearance of cowboys from a television series. They sway their shoulders and are always ready to draw their guns. The agent watches me nervously from the corner of his eye and asks Teelapon what I, a foreigner, am doing here. I follow Teelapon's advice, grab a broom and start to clean the office. A *phareng* cleaning woman! Never seen before! He doesn't have the courage to look at me any more.

I hurry away to take care of the little girls. In the state they are in, it is useless to begin asking them questions. We still have a lot of work to do to establish a few rules of basic psychology. No one, for example, is concerned about interviews given without any preparation right after a rescue. Thai journalists are allowed to come to the home and question the children! Result: we are left with children who are even more exhausted and depressed. All of this has to end. We will prepare dossiers, supply information and give the children's stories to journalists. But there is no question of any direct conversation with them. Just as in more advanced countries, it will be forbidden to question children who are victims of sexual abuse or ill treatment. It will take me months of arguing and explaining to get this code of ethics accepted.

At the end of a year's work the Center is functioning better than we could have hoped. The team has grown, the rescue home is practically always full and rescues continue at a good pace. We are now seriously planning to launch a program of prevention in the north of Thailand. According to our statistics, seventy percent of the children come from this region. A large proportion of them have had contact with tourists. AIDS has become one of our major worries. We see a net increase in children who are HIV positive. And security conditions have gotten worse. Teelapon was victim to an unusual aggression: in a brothel north of the city, the manager, about to be arrested, turned his bear loose. Attorney Teelapon was severely bitten and had to have seventeen stitches on his leg. Less incredible, Moo barely escaped a settling of accounts, and as for me, the anonymous phone calls have become a daily affair. They are always the same: insults, obscenities, or worse and even more agonizing, silence on the other end of the line. Nothing except the noise of breathing.

In Brussels, *Médecins sans Frontièr* has changed director of the program three times. One after the other, they come to see, and each time we must explain everything, show them everything. It is a little annoying. Happily, the last organizational bulletin said that the Regional Director, whom I know, is going to arrive. He is a competent man and I hope he will support our action. I am overloaded with work. As "coordinator" I have taken on part of the work at the home, supervision of the team and follow-up of cases. At the same time I continue my investigations in the bars and maintain contact with certain adult prostitutes. There is a lot of administrative work and bookkeeping with the partner foundation is complicated: bills in disorder are received in Thai, then they have to be translated and rewritten; I don't have a single day to myself, and whenever I do treat myself to a few days in Hanoi, I spend the time hunched over my computer.

Médecins sans Frontièr wants reports to be concise, François-Xavier Bagnoud insists I give them every little detail about each child; it is a real headache. The directors of the Center regret that they did not stipulate that one trimestral report would be given to all three partners: *Médecins sans Frontièr*, François-Xavier Bagnoud and the EEC. I just get finished with one report when it is already time to begin another. At the end of this first year I am also beginning to feel a certain moral fatigue. At night I wake up in a sweat, gripped with fear. I sleep with the light on. I don't dare mention any of this to Jean-Paul because I am sure he would ask me to quit. The anonymous phone calls are increasing. This week "they" called me every night. And always the same breathing at the other end of the line. I do not know who is behind this tactic, but I am certain my presence is a nuisance.

Nevertheless, the program is functioning better and better, the children are more and more numerous and we are soon going to initiate another home. *Médecins sans Frontièr-France* opened a logistics office a few months ago. The coordinator, a Frenchman in his thirties, is a little cold but dedicated. I have rented an office for the two of us and will have the benefit of a real secretary. I really need a place to work. I have had enough of travelling with my computer and my tons of paper. We will share this office for almost two years. I remember arriving one evening, completely discouraged. We had just lost a little girl eleven years old struck with AIDS. I had cried a lot and my eyes were so swollen it was impossible for me to hide it. We spoke about this case for a few minutes. I needed someone to listen to me. Nothing more. But all he could say to me was that I was fighting the impossible, that I would have suffered less working to feed the children in Mali. I let it go at that.

April 1991: the worst time of the year. The temperature is 101° and the humid heat sticks to your soul. Poo has received a phone call from a doctor, an anonymous phone call. The "doctor" was called to come to a family shop to take care of a worker who had been hurt, a little girl eleven years old whose finger had been cut off in a weaving machine.

When the doctor said the little girl had to be hospitalized urgently, the foreman refused: the little girl is a Laotian, a clandestine worker held prisoner in the workshop. The boss offered to buy the doctor's silence at a good price. The doctor accepted, but stricken with remorse, he immediately called the CPCR, gave the address of the workshop and hung up. The men at the Center quickly inform the police and the clandestine workshop is easily found: a Chinese building on the north side of Bangkok. Four children are freed including Yom the Laotian. Her finger is mutilated and she is immediately sent to the hospital where a graft is attempted. Yom leaves the hospital two weeks later. The graft is a partial failure: her finger will remain stiff and useless. The investigators of the CPCR find her Laotian family on the other side of the boarder where Yom was kidnapped. Poo accompanies the little girl back to her village. The reunion turns into a wonderful celebration at the village. Poo will take the opportunity to inform the people about the problem of kidnapping and false job agencies.

Child labor affects one hundred million children throughout the world, four percent of the world's potential labor force! During a stopover in Bangkok, Carlos Bauverd, an executive of the International Labor Office, listens to the stories of Yom the Laotian and many Thai children. He tells us that the ILO will soon launch an international campaign against child labor. His visit to the CPCR lasts only a few hours but it gives us a little hope and courage.

Spring is over, the heat has become torrid. Next month I will go back to Brussels for the association's general assembly. Jean-Paul should meet me there for a few days. This last week has been very busy. We have forty-two little girls at the rescue home, there are beds everywhere and the results of their physical examinations fall like sentences: twenty-two children - more than half - are HIV positive! Two of the teachers quit when they hear the results.

This is the first time that we have received such a badly infected group. The children are Thai, Burmese and Chinese from the province of Yunan. We are seriously beginning to wonder if a new traffic in children doesn't exist with China. The police authorities have given the CPCR the right to take charge of foreign girls. A first! Usually these girls are immediately sent to the immigration prison where they wait to be repatriated to Rangoon or Yunan.

These Chinese girls have a particular story. They left their villages with a work contract in hand, they walked by night for seventeen days across the countryside before reaching Thailand. During the march the smugglers accompanying them take the occasion to rape them. Once across the border they were sent by minibus to Chiang-Rai and Chiang-Mai. There the group was divided: the youngest were sent to Bangkok, the others were locked in a brothel for Thai at Chiang-Mai. Fifteen months of hell. I have never seen children in such a state of shock. In this case it is not a question of abuse but torture. The girls were regularly and savagely beaten with cudgels or leather straps. Their bodies show incredible signs of laceration, cuts more than twelve inches long and as always many burns.

The atmosphere at the home is terrible. The children cry all day. Just as we console one, another bursts into sobs. We cannot let them mix with the other children as usual. The girls stand in line to receive medicine or have their bandages changed by the two volunteer nurses who work with us every evening. What do the "crocodiles" and such refined people as Matzneff call all this? Oh, yes... "new love."

After the phase of despondency, the children become aggressive; the Chinese girls argue with the Thai and we go from one to the other. There are too many children, too many kinds of distress. We will need several weeks to get such a situation under control. As an emergency measure we decide to rent a house in Chiang-Mai. Three teachers volunteer to get the new home started.

Everything is calm and peaceful at the new home. Even better, local enterprises have agreed to give real vocational training to the girls staying at this second rescue home. Our action in Bangkok will continue to concentrate on emergencies. Team rotation must be assured so that everyone will know the difficulties but also the fantastic feeling of success when a child is reunited with her family.

As for me, I am on the go all the time. I only go home to fall into bed. I have given up my little Chinese house and taken a real Thai house in the same quarter. It took me only one evening to move. The whole team helped me to move my furniture and baskets. All in vain. The very first night the telephone rang six times. So they are spying on me, following my movements. I didn't close my eyes all night. Yesterday on the phone a man spoke in bad French. I think he was reading words he did not understand. He said I was going to die, burned in my new home.

No one was at the office and the house is made of wood. I locked myself in my room and called Teelapon but he was not home.

The silence in the house was unbearable. I thought I was going to go crazy, so I put on some classical music and tried to concentrate on Mozart's *Requiem*. At five o'clock, when day was breaking, I thought I had dreamed it all. The next night I was awakened by the sound of breathing; a man was sitting on the ledge of the outside window. I don't know what got hold of me, but I threw myself at him screaming. The man was so frightened, he fell. In the morning I found dried blood on the ground in the court. The man must have hurt himself when he fell. The neighbors spoke of burglary. When Teelapon heard what happened he had bars put on all the windows. The house is now protected, but from my bed I have the impression of being in jail. And if the house burns?

Of course the following night my anonymous caller again threatens to set the house on fire and emphasizes that the pretty bars on my house-prison are... perfect. That night Païthoon and his wife came to sleep in the guest room.

Fortunately nights come to an end and in the morning I go to the children's home. In the end things quiet down. The Chinese Consul in Bangkok, a brilliant and intelligent man, has finally understood the advantage of collaborating and negotiates with the authorities of Peking and Yunan for the repatriation of about thirty girls. For us it is out of the question to send them back without some guarantee. I am surprised that this rigid Chinese man in his fifties should have so much interest in our problem. He could easily demand unconditional repatriation from the Thai authorities. But he wants to see the CPCR succeed in its investigation of the networks that use children from his country. The explanation is simple: the new Thai government seems effectively to want to put an end to such wide-open corruption. Consequently, when a brothel is closed, if the girls are Thai, the managers risk a severe prison sentence. But Thai justice primarily wants to know if the young girls from the brothels are Burmese, Laotian or Chinese, in other words foreigners, because it considers them, first of all, as illegal immigrants. Proceedings against the brothel keepers drag and sometimes are lost. The time wasted permits an increase in traffic on the borders. That is why the Chinese Consul would like to see us finish our investigation: our reports will be helpful to his government in breaking the networks cropping up along the frontier.

Another tactic used by the procurers is a false home for children. An American named Mark Morgan, well-known with Interpol, is suspected of child commerce in the region of Chiang-Mai. This American, in fact, opened a rescue home for street children. We paid him a visit with the hope of collaboration. He seemed too evasive, too distrustful of us and we preferred not to work with such a dubious person. Afterward, the Thai press denounced his association with a network of Scandinavian pedophiles. Vacations had been organized for tourists to meet children from the home. The children boarding in the home described atrocious scenes. Two of the children were never found.

This case caused a wave of indignation in diplomatic circles and among non-governmental organizations. The organization pleaded innocence. If this traffic functioned so well, it was because he had connections with Thai and foreigners. It is ridiculous to try and make us believe that the American organized such a network by himself.

Work continues at the CPCR. We decide not to create a specific center for children that are HIV positive. It is not a question of finances; we do not want that kind of death house. For as long as it will be possible, we will try to re-integrate these children into their families. Better to die in a country village surrounded by her people than alone in a hospital, especially here. The exclusion and rejection of a girl that is HIV positive seems too much like being condemned to death. This principle is going to cause a lot of conflict. I now know the problems faced by the teams living with very ill children or children in a grave state of shock. Personally I would not do this kind of work; I do not want to take this elevator toward hell.

A few days later Teelapon prepares to leave for Yunan province in China. This evening the girls from the home have prepared a Chinese meal for us and decorated the garden with red lanterns and crepe paper. Some of the girls are embarrassed; they accepted work contracts unbeknown to their families. They had hoped to live the great adventure but found themselves in a Thai brothel. What will their parents' reaction be? Timidly the girls give us quantities of letters that Teelapon is asked to deliver. All of us dream of the moment when they can return to their country.

Attorney Teelapon drops me off at my house; we drink tea and chat until two o'clock in the morning. He asks if a watchman is guarding the house. I continue to think it is not necessary. We say good-night at the door, the car shifts into gear. I am alone. The telephone downstairs rings, a shiver runs down my spine. Not tonight! Leave me alone! I won't answer. The telephone rings forty times, then stops.

A second call follows the first. I pick up the receiver; always the same breathing. The room downstairs has windows on all sides that scare me. What if someone is outside? I run to my bedroom and lock myself in. The windows are locked and the blinds are down. From the outside "he" cannot see me in the room. This is the first time I fear the worst. I phone my colleague from *Médecins sans Frontièr-France*. No one answers. Attorney Teelapon hasn't gotten home yet and Païthoon the Prof is away up north. This time I am really alone. The telephone rings all night. Impossible to disconnect the cord. And to think that I didn't even have the presence of mind to leave the receiver off the hook! I cover the telephone with pillows and everything else I can find. Enough! I don't want to hear this ringing any more. I listen to the noises of the house and those outside. My heart starts beating very hard. Shh... Silence. I have the impression that someone is walking around the house. Something is moving by the window downstairs, the gate opens, closes, opens again. If I continue listening to each little noise, I'll be crazy by dawn. I feel like a prisoner in my own house. I fight with myself to keep from running to the door and leaping across the fifty yards that separate me from the house of *Médecins sans Frontièr* where Mrs. Tick would let me in. Fifty yards, not much normally but a lot if I am at risk. Am I falling into a trap? They didn't hesitate to beat me up and burn me the first time. How far would they go this time? I mustn't think about that. Jeremy says that bad things happen only if we think about them, but in his last letters he told me to be careful. Now I know what fear is. The more time passes, the more I feel vulnerable. I must resolve to wait for daylight.

My alarm clock shows six o'clock as the sun rises. My neighbors are already up and about. Like every morning, the old man coughs his heart out, his son leaves astride his *touk-touk*, the dog barks. I cannot see anything from my windows. There is no trace of my nighttime visitors. Was I just dreaming?

I turn the key in the lock and open the door to the courtyard. My God! What is that drawing of a body on the concrete with a bullet in the heart? And those inscriptions in Thai? The house cat has been nailed to the door. Fresh paint drips down the walls. Everything is blood red. Knives have been painted on the doors and windows. In the back of the house a fire has been prepared; all they need to do is throw in a match to set everything ablaze. My legs shake. This time it is very serious.

I call Teelapon, Sanphasit the Director and my colleague from *Médecins sans Frontièr-France*. In less than twenty minutes everybody is there. What are we going to do?

Teelapon and Sanphasit talk together. My Thai is still not good enough to understand everything, but it is clear that they are worried. Teelapon wants me to leave the house for a few days. Where would I go? My colleague from *Médecins sans Frontièr-France* is leaving for Laos tomorrow morning. I will have to call the head office and speak with them about it. Just three days ago our Regional Coordinator, Eric, was here. He would certainly have known what to do in such a situation. Above all, don't phone too quickly. Panic is a poor counselor. Teelapon wants me to go stay at the Foundation's village-school at Kanchanaburi for a week. He awkwardly tries to reassure me, repeating every two minutes that the incident is not very serious but immediately adding that it has become imperative to put a guard in front of my house and that I can no longer drive alone. The situation is beginning to irritate me: everyone wants to decide for me!

Suddenly the telephone rings. I stare at it. A simple phone ring terrorizes me. Teelapon picks up the receiver and hands it to me. It's Richard, a businessman I met during the Christmas holidays. He comes to see me when he passes through Bangkok. He came to live at Phuket three months ago. He plays tennis very well and loves boats. We went sailing together for two days at Christmas. A very nice guy and a lot of fun. Richard... Providence sent you to me.

I briefly tell him what happened. He suggests that I come to stay with him down south. The house is immense, there is a telephone from which I can call *Médecins sans Frontièr* and Jean-Paul. Teelapon welcomes this news with enthusiasm. I pack a few clothes, my toiletries bag, two files, my computer and I'm on my way out the door. Teelapon drives me to the airport. He has already reserved my ticket by radio. A one-hour flight later I am far away from this house covered with blood-red paint and its damned telephone.

In Brussels, Eric, the Regional Coordinator, wants me to leave the country. He wants to talk to Teelapon, hear what the Thais think. I ask him to promise to continue to support the follow-up of our action with *Médecins sans Frontièr* no matter what happens. I agree to return to

Europe to analyze the situation with them, but I want to come back. In the meantime I decide to spend a few days here at Phuket. I don't want to leave Thailand giving the impression that I am running away. Richard, true to his promise, lets me live at my own rhythm. This evening we are dining on the terrace:

- You know, Richard, I feel much better. I'm not even afraid anymore.

He turns red:

- Stop kidding me, will you? Who are you trying to fool? So you're not afraid anymore. Then how come you jump every time a motor scooter passes on the street? Why do you draw the curtains every time you go into a room? And when the telephone rings? Oh no, my sweet Marie, you're not afraid... but you're so jumpy I decided to leave the damned telephone off the hook! Marie, listen, you're scared to death. And it's nothing to be ashamed of.

I don't answer, but bury my nose in my napkin. He's right. I decide to go back to Brussels.

Attorney Teelapon is at the airport and we spend the day together. He tells me he has postponed his trip to China. My flight is at eleven p.m., direct to Brussels. I am leaving, but I will not abandon the program nor the team. I will be back in a month.

Païthoon the Prof has come to the airport to tell me good-by. He hands me the latest files and asks me to come back within the next few months. He calls after me:

- And don't forget the chocolate when you come back.

In Europe, the drama of the Kurds has just made the news. All the efforts of *Médecins sans Frontièr* are concentrated on this human tragedy. Thousands of people are fleeing from Iraq. The stories told by the teams there are horrible. Every hour children die of exhaustion, hunger and contagious diseases that spread with incredible speed. I can see that my problems of security will not be one of the main office's preoccupations. The urgency of Kurdistan, the daily routine of *Médecins sans Frontièr* and its general assembly overshadow my problems. When my program director returns from Iraq, he is overwhelmed by reporters and requests for financing from the EEC. We make at least three appointments to meet, but he is never able to make it. While I wait, I have the time to reflect. I am not the only one waiting. One after the other the Directors for Mozambique and Zaire come for news about their requests, without success. On the evening of my departure I am able to see the Director of Operations. The encounter lasts twenty minutes, barely enough to make it seem like a meeting.

I leave Europe asking myself why I came.

19.

PATCHARA, LAO AND THE OTHERS

This trip to Europe was useless! I am going back with empty hands and an empty spirit. It would have been better if I had stayed in Bangkok and waited for Eric to come back. Eric is the Medical Coordinator for *Médecins sans Frontièr* in Southeast Asia. He has been a constant support during these long months of work. Every time he passed through we discussed the difficulties encountered, the worst of which is, of course, the growing number of children who are HIV positive. I called Eric many times when I didn't know where to turn and he came every time no matter where he was, and every time he gave us his help. Our program is one of the most visited, but we must admit that the majority of these visits change nothing. Since Bangkok is a point of transit in Asia, most of the people from the head office of *Médecins sans Frontièr* feel obliged to pay us a visit. Among our visitors are people who never even imagined that children ten or twelve years old could be exploited in brothels, and they are stunned to discover the reality we have been speaking about in our reports for the past year. And there are still others who do not understand the project and confuse our work with Mother Teresa's. Not to mention professional photographers who don't find "anything interesting to film" in a rescue home for children but want to shoot footage in the brothels or in clandestine factories. Fortunately we never lose our sense of humor.

I am once again in my little house. Attorney Teelapon has hired a night watchman to keep guard in front of my door from six p.m. to eight a.m. and now I have a "beeper", a little gadget with which I can alert the team. And of course we changed the telephone number.

In Bangkok the rescue home is always full of children. The first group of Chinese girls is going to be repatriated and arrangements are progressing without any major problems. However, the team is going to send back to China only those children who are not HIV positive because it is difficult to foresee the Chinese government's attitude toward the problem of AIDS. Reporters say that there, carriers of the virus are systematically locked in special prisons; others mention a relatively tolerant attitude. Impossible to have an exact idea.

Yesterday evening thirteen little Thai girls arrived at the rescue home. The youngest ones, twelve years old, are Patchara and Lao, who are inseparable. I don't know it yet but these two little girls are going to have a special place in my heart. They are pretty girls with fine bones, long faces, and the dark skin of people from the north. They share the same room and are always cutting up, talking in a whisper way into the night. Mrs. Daeng, the nurse, is thinking about separating them. I advise her not to. This friendship is important; perhaps it will keep them from getting depressed as so often happens a few days after the child prostitutes arrive. Two members of our team are sick, so I am going to stay at the home for a few days. The days fly when I am with the children; there is always something to do. We begin classes for embroidery and silk flowers. They absolutely must be kept busy so they will not fall prey to depression.

A teacher comes to teach Thai every afternoon. Lao and Patchara have chosen this course. They study together and we listen to them recite the alphabet. Lao dreams of having a dressmaking shop in her village; Patchara already says they will work together. At least these two have projects, a big step toward their re-integration. Nine p.m.: this evening I will go over their lessons with them and take the opportunity to study the Thai manual I have been carrying in my bag since my return. The enthusiasm of these two little girls infects the whole group; however, something troubles me about Patchara. While she was taking her shower I noticed a large brown mark on her shoulder, something different from everything we have seen so far. It is not a burn but some kind of a thick scab that covers the skin in patches. I look through Mrs. Daeng's medical books but find no description of anything that resembles this mark. Since I will be taking all the children to the hospital tomorrow for a complete examination, I will speak to the doctor about this.

This evening the children are now in bed and the air has cooled agreeably. I have a cup of Chinese tea with Moodame, the teacher, then go to a table in the garden to write my last monthly report. The mosquitoes dance around me, a lizard, rigid on the chair, stalks its prey. I raise my head and see Patchara standing in front of the door. She is covered with sweat, big drops stand out on her forehead. I take her to the infirmary, her temperature is 101°. I examine the brown mark again. All of this indicates nothing good. I give her an aspirin and tell her to take a shower before going back to bed, but her mattress is soaked, unusable. I get another from the closet. Lao, sitting on her mat, is very uneasy. I reassure her with a few words in Thai, hang some insect strips for the mosquitoes and turn on the fan. I go to lie down on the wooden balcony but it is impossible to sleep, so I get up and walk around the garden. After a while, sitting on the swing, a feeling of discouragement overcomes me. I am filled with doubt and questions and this ever-present feeling of solitude that makes me dizzy. I miss Jean-Paul.

How much longer before I can meet him in Hanoi? Here, under the mosquito net on the balcony, a few of the children are sleeping, free. But tens of thousands of others remain locked in the brothels. They don't sleep. Our initiative is only a drop of water in the ocean. Perhaps my friends on the other side of the world are right. Should I resign myself, accept the fact that we will never be able to reverse the course of things? Must I forget the whole thing? I am tired of being afraid! Afraid of aggression, afraid also of not being able to do what this Thai team expects of me. On the other hand, the only thing they are lacking is money. For the rest they are quite capable of getting along without me. They are professionals. Am I at least helpful to them? And if, on the contrary, I am hindering their action with my problems of security according to Western standards?

Nevertheless, they consider me their equal, convinced that I will hold up to the end. I don't know if I will have the courage. They are sustained by their political convictions, their desire for liberty, while I have only the memory of Sonta to sustain me. On the balcony, Lao is restless. She is there like the others, physically but without any spirit. Suddenly I am sorry to have had such black thoughts. How can I quit now when the work has only begun?

The next day at the hospital our doctor friend does not hide his preoccupation. I understand from his half words that he suspects an already-developed case of AIDS and perhaps a syndrome of Caposis also, a skin infection the Thai develop which is particular to this part of Asia. There is something about the symptoms that do not resemble anything we know in Europe. We will have to wait for the results of Patchara's analyses.

Back at the CPCR ten boys from thirteen to fifteen have been freed from a clandestine paper factory. We have no place for boys this age. We ask a receiving center for street children to keep them while we look for their families and deal with the legal problems. These boys have been working fourteen months in this factory. They all show signs of maltreatment. Two of them have difficulty walking because of fractures that were poorly taken care of. Half of these children come from the northeast of Thailand, the other half come from the shantytowns around Bangkok. They ran away from their poverty thinking they would find something better in the capital. The job agents were waiting for them on the platform at the train station. The conditions they offered were tempting: a room, a salary and a regular job. Reality was different: ten children in a room, one tin bowl of rice a day, fourteen hours of work seven days a week, and a locked door. It was impossible to escape from this hell.

It is urgent that the tribes at greatest risk be alerted. Our program for prevention in the north must be developed. A team of four people originally from this mountain region tries to inform the village people about the networks of slavery. They carry a portable video around with them and show a film which tells a typical story of two children: one ends up in a brothel, the other in a clandestine factory. The film is based on the true stories of Sonta and a little boy and translated into various local dialects. The members of the team give instructive comic strips to the smallest children. They also observe the children who have returned to the village and make a record of new disappearances. Of course Yake the rebel remains the central figure of our preventive action in the northern region. He centralizes the information and sees that it is transmitted over the radio of Chiang-Rai. That way, the village people can help by reporting the presence of recruiting agents. Two weeks later the Chief of an Aka village and several of his men capture a woman who was offering fantastic work contracts to the community. This woman is a real prize which will make it possible to dismantle a network of eleven people.

Travelling, raids in Bangkok, searching for families, nights at the rescue home, visits to the hospital, writing reports, investigations in the bars... at this pace the months pass quickly.

20.

SOÏ COWBOY:
THE JAPANESE PACKAGE DEAL

Here it is June already and the rainy season has begun. The sky over Bangkok is covered with big gray clouds, the traffic becomes impossible and the storm sewers are overflowing from the tons of water that pour down on the capital every day. At Teelapon's request, I continue to frequent the bars. This is not my favorite activity, but it is true that we often glean some very good information.

My direction is *Soï* Cowboy, a street next to Sukhumvit Road. This *soï* has been competing with Patpong for many years. Prostitution is cheaper and less aggressive here. Many bars are reserved for the homosexual clientele. On this street, I met Bob, a fellow Belgian, a bearded man who arrived fifteen years ago in "Krung Thep", "the city of angels", as they say here.

Mr. Bob worked for fifteen years on a job site in Saudi Arabia where he discovered Asiatic charm from the Filipinos employed as domestics by the Arabs.

After that he married a Thai woman in order to have the right to own property in Thailand. According to Thai law, a foreigner cannot own more than forty-nine percent of a business, but this law can easily be got around by making recourse to silent partners. Hence, Mr. Bob is owner of three establishments: the Apache, the Ding Dong and the Quie Spot. He has a beautiful penthouse at the top of one of his buildings.

A sign openly advertises "Clean sex at Mr. Bob's."

According to him, the AIDS epidemic is very exaggerated, but all his girls are given a gynecological examination every week as well as an HIV test every month. Mr. Bob affirms that he has tried to convince the

girls to use condoms but was not successful. He recognizes that the
problem of women's slavery is very important, but of course not in his
bars! He is convinced that young women are fighting to come work in
his bars. It can also happen that Mr. Bob finds husbands from Germany
or France for the girls. He sighs: according to him, the Belgian
Ambassador in Bangkok does not collaborate enough. Every bit of
information is verified and requests drag on and on. The "males" get
tired of waiting and end up returning to their countries alone. So much
the better.

Mr. Bob has his preferences: he refuses to allow Arabs in his bars;
the girls complain about their violence. Mr. Bob prefers Europeans but
also appreciates the generosity of the Japanese.

Package deals, those trips where everything is included, is a nice
Japanese invention. In Japan, group activities are widespread and the
most productive executives earn a week's vacation in Thailand. The girls
are chosen from a catalogue and wait for their client in a hotel room.
Clean, easy, discrete.

- In general they change girls every evening. It can happen that they
organize parties with more than one girl, says Mr. Bob. I don't accept
this kind of session. The girls don't like it, but I rarely interfere. I let the
Japanese manage on their own. They pay very well.

One thing is certain: Mr. Bob makes a lot of money from *package
deals*.

At the beginning of the '80s European travel agencies also began this
type of service. In the bars of Bangkok you can still hear the tourists
referred to by the nickname "Neckermann" simply because certain
brochures distributed by this German company recommend hotels for
"travelers who want to go on a binge." According to information by
Chris De Stoop, a Belgian journalist who wrote a report about women's
slavery, the company Thailand Express in the Dutch village of Horn
distributed tourist brochures with pictures of young girls. Kanita Kamla,
a large tourist agency in Bangkok that specializes in sex vacations, wrote
in one of its brochures: "For 2,695 Florins or 8,000 French Francs:
ticket, room at the Dorchester Hotel and every evening the choice of six
little slaves. Every night at midnight, the guide will draw the name of a
girl for participants. The lucky winner will be able to share his bed with
two little pussycats." In the same brochure, Kanita Kamla mentions
so-called "cultural" information such as: "At twelve years old Thai girls

are raped by their fathers and instructed by their mothers about all sexual positions." And why not sodomized by the family elephant in their cradles? Poor Kanita Kamla, they don't know what other tales to tell to promote tourism.

Fortunately this kind of document is no longer on display at travel agencies but it continues to be passed discretely under the table by certain tour operators in the West.

Before leaving Mr. Bob's bar, I take the opportunity to talk with a little prostitute named Noy to check out what I have been told. Of course there is no screening for AIDS. Contraception and condoms are the girls' responsibility. They are not held illegally against their will, it's true, but their situation is not enviable, nevertheless. Almost all of them have a child in someone else's care in their village, and they earn barely enough to live on. This is the typical situation of prostitutes in Asia.

Just as I am about to leave, I am surprised to see Marc on the other side of the room. Marc, a nurse in his thirties, has been living between Pattaya, Bangkok and Paris for the last year. After having worked in a refugee camp, he went to rest in a *guest house* in Pattaya and practically never left. He works six months in Paris and comes back to Asia for six months. He knows all the girls on the coast and brags that he kisses a different one every night.

We have had dinner together three or four times in Pattaya. I have tried to talk to him about AIDS but he refuses to use any protection, convinced that there is no risk. He, too, says that the girls are clean and apparently in good physical condition. And he is a nurse!

I know from friends who work in the bars in Patpong that Marc also goes with children, little girls in a hotel on Suriwongse thoroughfare. Now I offer him a beer. He accepts. We leave the noise of the dance area and go to the terrace, which is almost empty. I look at him. He has gotten thinner. His eyes are bloodshot and almost yellow. I bluntly ask about his health.

He doesn't answer, looks away and changes the subject:

- I'm looking for a pad for the night, I'm broke. Can you put me up? My money will get here tomorrow with a friend from Paris.

- No, I don't want to have anyone stay at my house, but I can give you enough for a room and something to get by on for twenty-four hours. But then, you know how to get along.

We talk for three hours. He ignores the subject of AIDS. I tell him about the children at the CPCR. He tries to convince me that I am wrong. Once again I hear words that I know far too well:

- I love the children, I have never hurt any of them. You can't understand what they feel when I give them all this love. It's not the money I give them that's important, it's the tenderness before going back to the street. We can love children without beating them or even penetrating them. There are "games". They have expert hands, you know.

It is hot and Marc is sweating profusely. He takes off his cotton shirt; his shoulder and arms are covered with brown spots. I point to his shoulder:

- Hey! What's that?

His mask falls. He looks into my eyes and blurts out:

- I don't have to teach you the symptoms of this disease of the damned. I have AIDS and I am going to die from this shit. And believe me, I won't be the only one here!

-Shit! You're sick and you know it. And you continue to sleep around right and left with everyone? These kids never did anything to you. You don't have the right to contaminate them for vengeance.

- And me? What did I do to deserve this? I'll be thirty years old next month and I know I am going to die here! Alone!

-We can help you go back to France, to get treatment so you'll suffer less. We can contact a member of your family, a friend. Listen...

I'm wasting my time. He has already gotten up. I know that my arguments are weak, but what can I say to him? He gambled, he lost. And it is still unjust to see a man condemned to AIDS no matter what he did.

He leaves the table, goes to the bar and talks to a girl. They leave together. A crime seems to be hanging in the air, the one that Marc is about to commit with this prostitute.

I leave too and go home; there'll be no sleeping tonight. I have been talking to Marc for months about AIDS and the possibility of contamination. I can still hear him laughing at me. He, a nurse, a health specialist, continued to make love without a condom, without protection. And now, condemned to death by his negligence, why does he continue to sleep with scores of women, girls and children? Out of desperation or hate? To drag toward death with him as many people as possible, innocent people who, before dying, will kill others! What a vicious circle!

Once again I think of Alain, all the things he said, his favorite books. I have read the latest book by Gabriel Matzneff, who tells in an intimate diary, his sexual adventures in Manila with very young Filipino children. Excerpts:

"During my many visits to the Philippines I have known all sorts of children: certain ones seem to be passionately attached to me, others pretend to be attached to worm some pesos out of me; but I have also known children - and I remember in particular a young girl of fourteen who was introduced to me by Jean-Jacques D. - who, while we were making love, asked me impatiently every two minutes: It's finished?, which in French we would say: *'Alors ton coup, tu le tires oui ou merde?'*" page 249, "My Analysed Loves". He continues:

"...At Robinson's I was alone and melancholy; the young people who winked at me were all little whores of the worst kind, girls and boys, most certainly infected, not very appetizing. I left when a fresh, charming boy, whom I thought to be a girl at first, stared at me. It was a good choice, as Giscard would have said; yes, a pretty boy, bubbling with mischief, speaking good English, a clean schoolboy, thirteen years old. He didn't want me to kiss him, but he sucked me marvelously and made me come. (...) Afternoon, "love" with a little rose, fourteen years old. She was a real little savage who brushed her teeth with after-shave lotion and cleaned her shoes with the washcloth. In bed, this little rosebud let me undress her with sensuality and ardor. (...) Amorously, what I experienced in Asia is very inferior to what I experienced in France even if the little eleven or twelve-year-old boys that I put in my bed are a rare spice. Yes, a spice, but only a spice: a spice and not the main dish."

The intimate diary of Gabriel Matzneff is 435 pages of descriptions of this kind. Sometimes he tells about his afternoons watching films in which the actors are younger than fourteen:

"Afternoon watching child pornographic movies at JCG's house. I am familiar with some of his films because I saw them in Dijon at the home of unhappy Jacques S. He sent them to JCG a few days before committing suicide. Out of the dozen films he showed me - private films very superior to those in series sold in Amsterdam or Denmark - at least three were exciting, lovely: a thirteen-year-old girl and two boys her age, two boys of twelve and thirteen, three boys from ten to fourteen all fondle each other, suck each other, take each other, do pussycat and rose petal, etc. It was delightful, but once again it was clear to me that I am not a spectator: what I love is to live it, not watch others live it."

Matzneff is not writing a book of fiction, he is reporting real facts, the hours he passed with children in Asia between 1983 and 1984.

He writes, gives speeches, and talks at length on TV talk shows. No one protests.

When another author dared to tell Matzneff on live TV that his pedophilia was disgusting as well as a crime, some intellectuals retched. In the magazine *Le Monde*, in an article entitled "Who's Afraid of Gabriel Matzneff?", a journalist indignantly wrote, in the name of literature and freedom of expression: "When magazines make "dossiers" to find out if "literature can say everything," it is time to start worrying. And when repeated crimes of racism make less of a noise on television and disturb the morals of charitable women less than the numerous, voluptuous, tender and altogether insignificant loves of a very pacific man, it is urgent to worry."

The article was concerned only about the pedophilic writer's adventures with "...very young girls, fifteen, sixteen or seventeen years old." The only thing it forgot to mention was that Matzneff, when speaking in the Philippines, speaks about eleven-year-old children, but by some strange coincidence, when speaking in Paris, mentions only young women of an age that would not land him in court. Sixteen in Europe but ten or twelve in Asia. Come on! Those who protest must be really "charitable women", idiots, read critics with reactionary tendencies, therefore dangerous. A little bit of mixing up, some looking the other way and a lot of hypocrisy. I will often hear the lame excuse: "Who's afraid of Gabriel Matzneff?" No one. Except, perhaps, the children when he lays down his pen.

Matzneff is a public figure. By allowing him to speak in broad daylight about his sexual abuse of children without doing anything to stop him, means giving pedophilia a platform, permitting sick adults to sexually abuse children in the name of literature. Then what good is it to fight against the traffic of children or against magazines that use little kids six, seven or eight years old for pictures? The little girl the writer sexually abused is just like the children encountered hundreds of times in Bangkok.

In France, an adult might testify, there may be a trial. In Asia, a child prostitute is nothing more than an item of consumer goods; he does not count. In publishing his diary, Matzneff not only tramples on the rights of Asian children but on the rights of all children as well. His intimate diary was published in 1990, the same year France ratified the Convention for Children's Rights. Double talk.

It is narratives like Matzneff's that feed the phantoms of men in search of children. Theories such as theirs permit Alain the architect to nourish his pathology and to believe that he loves the children he leaves in the morning in a hotel room in Bangkok, Saigon or elsewhere. They are all links in the chain: those who kidnap the children, those who buy them, those who, like Matzneff and his brothers, deceive them. All of them are part of the same foulness. What difference is there between the Chinese man at the Suriwongse Hotel and Gabriel Matzneff? None, in fact. Both of them negotiate the life of a little girl, one for money, the other to sleep with her. Children disappear every year in Europe, kids that will never be found, who probably supply the networks of pedophiles. Thousands of false tourists walk the sidewalks of capitals like Rio, Manila, Colombo or Bangkok looking for children. Publishing houses, knowing full well what they are doing, publish addresses for pedophiles. International clubs have been organized to bring together these followers of "new love". Harmless love? The child who does "pussycat and rose petal", which he wrote so nicely about, is the same child we find later lying on her mattress soaked with sweat. At the best, all she has to contend with are her nightmares; at the worst, her bouts of fever are caused by abdominal pain, canker sores, lung infections or the brown spots on her body. This is the future a child infected with AIDS. Today we know all this.

I didn't sleep last night. I ended up watching an American police movie on the video. The same film kept playing for hours until the night ended. Until I was exhausted.

I am drinking my third cup of strong coffee this morning; the bus for the CPCR is waiting for me. At the rescue home life continues its course. Some thirty girls live here together until their families can be found and their injuries begin to heal and they begin to think about their future.

New children arrive, other children leave us to go back home. We become attached to the children as we face every problem together. We, too, must accept the limits of what we can do. We must stop feeling guilty every time AIDS is diagnosed; as Brussels says, we must "rationalize". They are right, but it's not that simple.

Patchara and Lao are sitting on the swing in the garden. They love to play here, swinging together as if they are rocking each other. Patchara is sick, the infection is advancing at lightening speed. I haven't seen her for three days and in that time her condition has gotten worse. She is losing weight irreversibly. The psychologist spends hours trying to get her to eat strengthening foods and drink sweet drinks, but her mouth is covered with small blisters and herpes. Every mouthful makes her suffer terribly. The hospital's prognosis is very bad. The medical personnel wants no contact with her and in half words they make us understand that they refuse to take care of her. Our doctor friend does not know how to justify his team's behavior. It is quite simple: like all of us, they are afraid of death. And Patchara is a little girl that is going to die. We all know it. I would like to be able to refuse that, too.

Sometimes I say to myself that I am incompetent and useless because I, too, am afraid. But at other moments I am proud that I cannot accept seeing a child die. I had this same feeling when I worked at the hospital in Brussels five years earlier, a feeling of rebellion that will never leave me.

March 11, 1992: Patchara is dead.

Patchara died last night. She went out like the flame of a candle in the small hours of the morning. The news hit me like a slap so violent that I can still feel it burning my cheek. I would like to believe, like my Thai colleagues, that the spirits have carried her to heaven and that some day she will come back in another form. Patchara is dead and Lao's hopes, and mine, died with her. I am at the end of my resources, incapable of accepting this latest death, this defeat of life. I have stayed in bed the whole day listening to the tape of *Petit Prince* over and over, never answering the telephone. The air conditioner blows out its glacial breath and the cold reminds me of the winters at home in Europe, far from this horror.

Go back to Europe! Leave Thailand. Return to Brussels and see Jean-Paul again, my family and the hospital. Have a normal life. Night has fallen with its trail of anxiety. I have emptied my closets, folded my clothes and packed my suitcases. Tomorrow, first thing, I will get an airline ticket to Brussels. I have cleaned the house to make it easier for my friend Païthoon to move my things. And I took a sleeping pill.

When I wake up my watch indicates ten o'clock and the sunrays shining through the blinds make shadows on my bed. It is late. At the CPCR, Attorney Teelapon must be worried about my being late. I go downstairs, pass my suitcases in the hall without daring to look at them and make straight for the bathroom. I must hurry.

- Mally! Open up!

Teelapon and Païthoon bang on the door.

I open it. Teelapon trips on my suitcases and looks at me dumbfounded. Païthoon blocks my way:

- You don't have the right to leave! Not without telling us. Not without saying goodbye. Not you, Mally...

This is the first time that the "Prof" has spoken to me so harshly. Teelapon grabs my two suitcases, climbs the stairs and throws them on the bed. He scowls. In a cutting voice that allows no appeal he tells me to prepare a small bag and take a few days vacation in the home of a Thai family.

Whose?

- Why mine, naturally! answers my faithful friend.

In the garden at the rescue home, Lao sits for hours on the red swing. Alone.

All her projects and dreams have disappeared with Patchara. They had dreamed of sharing the same dressmaking shop, of visiting their families together, of growing up hand in hand. Now, pensive, she continues to study Thai, doing her lessons on this same swing. Sometimes she talks to herself in her room. When that happens, the other children try not to bother her. We find out a short time later that Lao, too, is infected with AIDS.

21.

A TRIP TO CHINA

I have been waiting for this week-end. My friend Hans arrives tonight from Brussels. I say friend because I feel that is what he is, but in truth I hardly know him. We lived in the same four-storey building in Brussels along with an old mysterious watchmaker, a brilliant couple of university students, and Antoine, a Greek hypnotizer.

I felt immediately at home in this building. Jean-Paul and I visited the apartment with a flashlight one evening and bought it right away.

Two days later he left for Vietnam and I moved in by myself on Sunday afternoon. The movers were dragging in boxes and furniture when a young man came in and offered me a cup of coffee. Dutch tradition wants that neighbors prepare drinks and sandwiches at such times. When I left Brussels to return to Bangkok, Hans offered to take me to the airport. We wrote to each other a few times and now he is coming to spend four days in Bangkok. I'm glad.

The CPCR takes up all my life, so Jean-Paul's visits to Bangkok or week-ends visiting him in Hanoi help to recharge my batteries. Twenty-four hours of happiness against fifteen days of horror. Fortunately there are occasional everyday pleasures, contact with the children, and the team.

I am glad to see Hans. We walk along the canals in the old section. Païthoon, like a real "Prof", wrote on a piece of paper, in Thai, the best places to visit: the Chinese market and its pagodas embalmed with incense, small typical restaurants. We shop in silk boutiques and stroll through Jim Thompson's to find little gifts for everyone in the apartment building in Brussels. A short visit but a big breath of fresh air. I needed it.

Lao has been driving us crazy these last few days. This little girl is so changed. She avoids all contact, all conversation, and assailed Mrs. Daeng, the nurse, calling her a liar in front of everyone. To lose face in Asia is the worst thing that can happen to someone, and Mrs. Daeng broke down in tears. She, too, is psychologically exhausted. Everyone here is at the mercy of weakness. Lao shouts at anyone who will listen that the doctor made a mistake, that she is not sick. All we can do is wait patiently for her to calm down. And begin all over again.

Tell or not tell the truth about AIDS? It is easier not to say anything. But the risk of contamination really does exist. The children return to their villages and we must warn the others. Even if I doubt that in the villages up north they use condoms, we have to make a stake for the future. We are obliged.

The days pass quickly and it is already June. This morning I went to the office of *Médecins sans Frontières-France* where I ran into Frédéric Laffont and Stéphane Thiollier, two reporters from the agency *Interscoop* in Paris. They will be here for about ten days making a report about the on-the-spot teams of *Médecins sans Frontières*. They have been working on this project for almost two years now, but they have never heard anything about our action. This is not surprising. Our little project is drowning under a flood of catastrophes. I am a little sorry that I upset the two of them this morning when they spoke to me about refugees. I was in a hurry and thinking about the little Chinese girls, our continuous daily problems and Lao. Even so, two minutes were enough to understand that they are not false firebrands but real professionals.

Frédéric and Stéphane returned to France shocked by what they had seen and heard. They called me regularly after that, long phone calls that helped me to resist. They talked to everyone around them about our project. We began to exist officially. Their visit lasted twenty-four hours, but it changed our daily life. Later, Frédéric will become a member of the Board of Directors of *Médecins sans Frontières-France* and will continue to support our project. We are a little less alone.

July, August and the rainy season. September and the first blue skies. October, November and trips to the villages of the Akha and Lishu tribes. The days are too short and the nights of insomnia are filled with anonymous telephone calls. We are rescuing more and more Chinese children, girls from eleven to fourteen, kidnapped or looking for work in factories and rescued from the most infamous brothels of Chiang-Rai.

The commerce in children extends to the borders with Burma and China. A gigantic octopus whose tentacles have momentarily loosened their hold on Thai children to attack new victims. The networks have always functioned according to demand and supply. Clients left the Philippines for children of Sri Lanka; now they are in Bangkok and Pattaya in Thailand, tomorrow in Vietnam or Cambodia.

This evening I have been invited to John's, whom I haven't seen for many months. Nothing has changed in the apartment. The Chinese pottery is still very beautiful, the canopy has been redone with cotton cloth from Bali. I remember the time spent here with Toy. Three years have passed and I never saw him again. The smell of hot peppered fish soup comes from the kitchen. This soup is a Thai specialty improved upon by my friend John. John is still working between Bangkok and Hong Kong and now also in Vietnam. We spend a very nice evening together but John carefully avoids speaking about our action and child prostitution. We say good-night about 11:30 p.m. I promised a young prostitute at Patpong that I would bring her some condoms and contraceptives. I ask John to come with me and to have a last drink. He declines the invitation, claiming he is tired.

At Patpong I see my friend behind the counter; I pass her the package and a card from the CPCR. I wave my hand and leave. The street is jammed with people, tourists buying imitations of Cartier, a group standing in line at the Pink Panther to see the week-end show. I catch sight of Attorney Teelapon and Moudame the psychologist on the other side of the street. Moudame suggests we look into a new dive. The place is detestable and packed with people. I have had enough and Teelapon suggests we leave. We cross Patpong. In front of a bar, a young Thai calls out to Teelapon, talks for a few moments and asks him to come in. I follow Teelapon inside... and my blood freezes.

Sitting on a stool facing the counter, John is holding a teenage boy of about fifteen on his lap. The man and the boy caress each others bodies. I don't want to believe it.

Teelapon pulls me by the hand to the middle of the room. John sees me and gets up quickly. He crosses the room and we stand there face to face. He stammers words I don't hear. I want to flee. I saw what I saw: John sitting on a stool at the bar with a boy in his arms. Memories come scrambling to my mind. I can hear Toy's words, "You are wrong about John, Mally", Virginia's warning, and the letter John wrote me from

Hong Kong asking me to forgive him. Why didn't I see all these signs, or rather, why didn't I want to see them? Why was I deaf and blind to his sometimes strange behavior? I would probably have distrusted a vulgar man with crude language and an unshaven face, but not John, a friend, a colleague. We have similar careers, mutual friends, the same interests, the same desire for change. Both of us fight for a better world. He is a pedophile, too. The idea is unbearable. Why did he act out this comedy for me? Like all the pedophiles I have met, he has two lives. The minute I saw John like that, I touched bottom. Since the beginning of my work here, it has been hard for me to accept the idea that a man can come to feel this desire for a child. I have lost my friend. Worse, I have the impression that I will never be carefree again. Something inside me has broken definitively. After John, my outlook on the world will never be the same again.

Teelapon's hand leads me toward the exit. My body follows him like a rag doll. The days that follow are painful. "You are wrong, Mally..." Toy's phrase haunts me. He understood right away that John was lying. I was blinded by my feelings; I didn't see a thing.

Jean-Paul is in Bangkok.

A few months ago we decided to get married in Asia. After several administrative problems, a date is finally set. On November 21, 1991 the Belgian Ambassador quickly reads the required phrases. Twelve minutes later I have learned that I now have access to Jean-Paul's bank account! The Ambassador preferred to speak of the "family funds". People have definitely lost their sense of romanticism. A glass of champagne and one last question from the Ambassador: where exactly is the "place of mutual residence" that characterizes all marriages? I explain to him again that I am not going to live in Hanoi and that my husband is not going to live in Bangkok! The Ambassador looks at us completely disillusioned. He starts to talk to us about marriage annulment, but we are already outside, walking hand in hand. Today is a holiday! Tomorrow Jean-Paul will go back to Hanoi and I will go to China. We will have our honeymoon two months later. A wonderful trip to New York even though it is freezing, minus three degrees Fahrenheit!

Right now the team is flying to Yunan, taking eleven little Chinese girls with us. These girls are returning to their country after eighteen months of forced prostitution. Three of them are HIV positive. We have

worked many months with the Chinese Consul in Bangkok to find their
families and put together each child's story.   At the airport, Chinese
officials are waiting for us.   The Chief of Police and all his men are
present, long speeches are made and toasts of friendship.   Outside the sky
is gray and the thermometer shows 20° F. My Thai friends are dressed as
if they were going to the North Pole.   They look funny bundled up in
sweaters and warm coats.   The children stand in a tight group behind us;
joy and anxiety are evident on their faces.   Officers examine each photo,
verify papers and stamp them.   We wait almost two hours in this
washed-out tiled hall before we are transferred, the children in minibuses
and the Thai delegation in police cars.   The Chinese stare at me with
curiosity. We are going to spend ten days in a little town in the province
of Yunan.   The children's parents have crossed the country to reach us
each in the hope of finding their child.   They spent hours making
declarations, signing papers and going from one office to another, but
they are here to welcome their child and take her back to their village.

The little girls are laughing and crying at the same time. We watch
them leave in old Soviet busses. Hands wave, another life begins.

We have many meetings and official visits during the day, but in the
evening we take the opportunity to visit this mysterious country.   The
three members of the team spend hours eating in the markets; they taste
everything including *"canards déshabillés"*, lacquered ducks.   I stroll
through the narrow streets buying quantities of Chinese brushes, rice
paper and Mao caps. I nibble on tofu of a thousand aromas and try to
memorize the odors and sounds of this country.   There are bicycles
everywhere, their bells singing, old people sitting on little benches
coughing their phlegmy cough and clearing their throats.   Incredible
China. I pass three very old women, their tiny feet tucked into black
velvet slippers. Old men dressed in ink blue working clothes, the last
image of Mao's Communism, stroll on the wide boulevards.   Movie
billboards are hand painted with the bland faces of actors from Hong
Kong. We are staying in a small hotel that the authorities have put at our
disposal. The nights are cool and hot water is rare. From my room I can
see a row of small houses. The workers who live there seem like ants in
perpetual activity. Thick smoke rises from the chimneys and the autumn
wind spreads the delicious smell of noodle soup.

This morning we accompanied Tchou to her hometown. This girl is
thirteen years old but looks much younger. Tchou escaped from the
brothel where she was kept prisoner by passing through a ventilation

duct. Tchou, an expert in Chinese gymnastics and incredibly supple, slipped into the duct during the night and climbed noiselessly to the outside. As soon as she was free, she ran to the nearest police station. Luckily she knows a few words in Thai and the police officer, with whom we have worked in the past, contacted us right away. Tchou's testimony brought about the rescue of thirteen children and twenty-one young women.

Tchou's parents are craftsmen who make natural colors for dying cloth. Her father works in his small courtyard mixing plants and bark to obtain a colored powder. His wife dyes pieces of cloth that she hangs to dry on long lines crossing the street. This tiny frail woman with gray hair welcomes us at the door. Tchou, several feet behind us, observes her parents' reaction. We watch, touched, her reunion with her mother and father. And we leave. Tchou doesn't need us anymore.

Back in Bangkok, we return to our daily routine of meetings, evenings at the home, and administrative reports. Now we have two rescue homes, both full of children. There is never enough room, but we do not want to create other homes. Thai associations must take over and create other receiving facilities for children in difficulty. I greatly admire the committee members of the Children's Center. Their participation is not limited to offering large sums of money; they also examine possible strategies of action.

In December 1991 I receive a surprising call from Paris. Reporters from the magazine *Elle* were present at a press conference held by *Médecins sans Frontières-France,* which was celebrating its twentieth anniversary. Three fifty-minute programs were televised to commemorate this event: the reports made by Frédéric and Stéphane. Thailand and the child prostitutes were the last of the series. Ten minutes of strong images, the expressions on the children's faces and the voice of Michel Piccoli, who spoke about the last slavery of the 20th century. The press conference room in Paris was dead silent.

The Editors of *Elle* want to give me the Woman of the Year Award 1991, a symbolic title. I do not understand why this sudden interest, but I hope it will help to end our isolation of the last two years. The reporters Patricia Gandin and Marie-Françoise Colombani, shocked by the contents of the report, have decided to move heaven and earth to bring the truth out into the light of day. *Médecins sans Frontières-France* discovered on a small television screen the battle we have been leading against the enslavement of Thai children. The infernal machine of the media has gotten carried away and talks about nothing else except our action. Pressure is building and the phone rings every two minutes, but there is no reaction from Brussels. I am leaving for Paris for a few days of press conferences, interviews and several meetings.

I have the unpleasant impression that I am being manipulated. There are already rumors about things I never said and sometimes never even imagined. My interest in such a project is questioned: concern for morals or defense of children's rights. Always the same old useless controversy. One thing is certain: the subject bothers a lot of people. It is cheaper to call someone moralist or fanatic in order to hide the reality of the question.

Some people, like Xavier Emmanuelli, Frédéric, Stéphane and a few others want to force the association to speak out. Newspapers and magazines publish articles that are mostly true stories, modest but strong, but some articles are published just to create a sensation, and this fills me with shame. Everyone wants to interview child victims, visit clandestine factories and participate with the police in rescues from the brothels. Hey, sure! Nothing could be more simple. Of course this is not possible. I also met reporters who, three months earlier, were still laughing at this project. Now they are acclaiming it from the rooftops. Things have certainly changed. A reporter from a scandal magazine in Paris wants to stay side by side with us for three weeks and investigate the network regarding children... under six. A scoop, as she calls it. I refuse this kind of visit. Some become angry, others try to convince us or act as victims. One television program wants a Thai girl to come to their TV station and speak on their program. I know how my team feels about this: the answer is no.

Back in Bangkok reporters come bursting unannounced into the offices of *Médecins sans Frontières* and the CPCR. I wonder if we are having a bad dream. I have no experience with these kind of people.

I will never forget one scene. I was alone in the office of *Médecins sans Frontières*. Mrs. Tick, the cleaning woman, had prepared Chinese tea. There was mail to go over, faxes and telephone messages and many appointments scheduled for the day. A bearded man about forty came in and in a bumptious voice announced that he was an important reporter from a very famous French magazine. In less that three minutes he had established "our" program for the next forty-eight hours. What? Without even asking, he thought I was going to agree to waste precious time making a round of the brothels with him in exchange for having my name in his article. Our collaboration ended right there but he pestered me for three days.

Fortunately, we also met real journalists, professionals who listened and verified all information. Kind men and women capable of carrying on their own investigation, who respected all the work done by the team. Many of them became true friends, who later helped us to present our findings in Europe.

Thanks to the Woman of the Year Award we began to exist with international and Thai authorities. Our fight against child slavery had come out of the closet and into broad daylight. As for me personally, I became the object of people's admiration but more so of their jealousy and rivalry. I made new friends; I also lost many. The least little error, the smallest *faux pas*, were objects of criticism. So what! No one can take away from me what I lived through.

In December several sections of *Médecins sans Frontières* decide to launch a campaign of information with travel agencies. This was an interesting idea proposed by an ex-director of a travel agency who now works for *Médecins sans Frontières-Switzerland*. In practice, only the Swiss branch carried out this project. Posters were hung in travel agencies, which promised to add an information letter to every ticket bought for Bangkok. This campaign, directed by Paul Vermeulen, was a success. Three months later agencies were asking for more of these information letters. In Bangkok, we received more than six hundred letters of support in less than one month. Ambassadors from various countries actively collaborated to support this campaign.

Micheline Pelletier's photographs appear in *Paris-Match*, which also publishes pictures of the project in northern Thailand, of the village-school in Kanchanaburi and of children swimming in the River Kwai. Pretty pictures, say the Thai. A local magazine publishes these same photographs along with part of the written article, but when they appear, a new wave of criticism "crosses" the ocean. I have enough of this nonsense! Now I am accused of a lack of reserve with the children and of flirting with my coordinator, Attorney Teelapon! I will have to find the strength to laugh it off, like Jean-Paul. But the members of our team are shocked at such Western rivalry. Once again, Teelapon,

Sanphasit the director, and their colleagues will do everything to see that
this criticism does not harm me. Fortunately this new attack came during
the visit of a reporter from the *Nouvel Observateur*. We work together
for almost two weeks. I was very reticent in the beginning. We were
having a lot of problems in our two rescue homes with children in the
terminal phase of AIDS, Lao in very bad condition and the team on its
knees from fatigue. We were all very tired, and the idea of receiving one
more journalist didn't help the situation. We had organized a vacation
camp down south for the children, and while they were away we used the
time to repaint the walls and freshen up the houses. The journalist
arrived as scheduled and we spent a lot of time together at the various
sites of the project. We visited Yake's home in the north and for the first
time I was able to forget all the solitude I had felt during these years at
the CPCR, being abandoned by the people of my own culture and being
labeled a moralist and a religious fanatic. I spoke to him for many hours
about this big adventure with my Thai friends, told him everything about
my fears, this life in constant turmoil, the anonymous phone calls and the
need to have a permanent night light. That night I went to sleep freed of
all these anxieties. By morning I had drawn a conclusion from my
confession: I decided to leave Thailand the following September, six
months later. I went for a walk up the mountain with Teelapon and I told
him my decision. Attorney Teelapon took me by the shoulders:

- You won't really be leaving us, Mally. Help us over there in
Europe. Help us to find new financial support, to convince the EEC that
traffic in children does exist in Asia.

My reply, of course, was yes. We continued walking. He smiled:

- I must say that I never thought you would stay with us all this time.
I will never forget all the moments shared together.

Nor will I, they are unforgettable.

The reporter from the *Nouvel Observateur* returned to France but we
kept in touch by telephone and mail. I told him confidentially that I have
not felt very safe in Bangkok for the last few weeks. The media in
Thailand and other parts of Asia have published information concerning
my presence in this project. Anonymous phone calls and threatening
letters are so numerous that the watchmen quit one after the other.
Sometimes I sleep at the office of *Médecins sans Frontières*. Once, after
my return from a ten-day trip up north with the team, the maid went into
a panic when she found a package in front of the door that contained

scraps of meat and a message in the form of a question glued to the inside cover of the box: "Are these human or animal?" A knife was stuck through them. "A threat to take seriously," said the Thai.

Three packages arrive in less than a week. Neither the neighbors nor the watchman can explain how these packages reach the door. The last one was hung on the shutter of my bedroom. I don't sleep anymore. Yesterday evening I went to a bar at Patpong, a place managed by a Frenchman whom I know. This time he was very aggressive and accused me of ruining his business with my campaigns of information and my stand on AIDS. When I left the bar, the marks left by his fingers were still visible on my right arm. He caught up with me on the street and pointed to a big Chinese with an unpleasant face that was with him:

- If you continue this nonsense, he will take care of you, and I wouldn't wish that on you!

Fear is my constant companion, never leaving me for a single moment.

A few days later another package comes to the house. Teelapon opens it. It is oddly light, empty, except for a knife with a sharp blade and a message in Thai and English: "Will you be the next package?" said the white paper spotted with red liquid.

I call *Médecins sans Frontières* in Brussels and then Jean-Paul in Hanoi to tell them that I have decided to leave Thailand sooner than planned. It will be better for me and for all those who want me to leave. My friends will take care of my personal belongings and the house. It is a terrible feeling to leave in defeat.

For the first time I have the impression of abandoning my team, the children, Lao and all the others. Teelapon and Païthoon drive me to the airport. We are not prepared for this separation.

22.

GOODBYE TO BANGKOK

Sitting on the back seat, I let the memories run through my mind. I remember my arrival in Asia in 1986: I was twenty-five and looking for adventure! I remember the goodbyes at the airport in Brussels and my first walks around Bangkok. I wanted to see everything, do everything; I thought I understood Asia. With the tips of my fingers I touched lightly upon its culture, its people and their history. But above all I learned to know myself. I had believed for a long time that I was afraid of solitude, but I overcame it. I discovered that it was enough to want something very much to find the strength to accomplish it. That everyone can move mountains if he lets the child inside him come out. It's true, mine was particularly turbulent. She never grew up and is still there. There is certainly something in my background that makes the disappearance of a child intolerable. I believe, Grandmother Simm, that I understand a little better what it is. I would never have gotten used to the barbed wire environment of the Vietnamese and Cambodian refugee camps, to the brutal presence of the Thai soldiers and their anger. And when I found out that the children were taken away to supply the networks of prostitution, I refused to allow myself any philosophical reflection and I let my heart speak. This anger sustained me for four years.

Sonta was the little light that guided me down this chaotic path. She was what kept me from quitting and packing my bags. When she died, in the spring of 1991, surrounded by her family but without me, there in her mountains, I still could not bring myself to abandon everything. And then there was Lao and Patchara and so many other, those little flames that I saw return to their villages or die. They gave me the strength to continue.

I left my friend Toy two years ago on a sidewalk in Bangkok. It was lunch time and the street was jammed with people. He kissed my cheek and slipped into a taxi; a wave of his hand and then... nothing. Not a single word after that. If I am sad it is not because I never saw him again but because I did not understand the reason for his silence. The worst thing is not to know why someone disappears. I am still living with this enigma today.

Meeting the pedophiles, Alain, Nicolas, Helmut and the others were extremely difficult moments for me. I hated them before comprehending the illness they carry inside them. I will never accept what they do but I can consider the possibility of treating them and a program of prevention. With John, my friend, the traitor, I thought that I had definitely lost the strength to continue, and I felt a pain in my heart. And then there is everything achieved with Attorney Teelapon, Païthoon the Prof, Sanphasit the director and the team of the CPCR, the important moments, the times of crisis and the celebrations, the visits to the village-school of Kanchanaburi or to the home of Yake the rebel chief in the mountains to the north, the nights spent talking around a kerosene lamp, the trip to China and its odors. All of this is written in the hundreds of pages of my diaries, an adventure that I set down on paper so I would never forget any of it. Every detail is there. I know that I can once again smell the odors of the markets, hear the sound of musical instruments and the jingling of the metal rings the giraffe women of Burma wear around their necks. In Thailand I lived through the most difficult moments of my existence: I felt abandoned and judged, afflicted by illness and torture and the specter of AIDS and death. I also experienced extraordinary moments: the liberation of the children, the successive victories against the tentacles of the Chinese Mafia, and the unconditional affection of the whole team, who never deceived me, never betrayed me. The names in my address book have changed; I have crossed out some and others have been lost, but those that remain or have been added to this maroon-colored book will never be crossed out.

It is time to say goodbye to my Thai friends. We have come a long way together, doing the best we could. In any case I prefer to regret our errors rather than have the remorse of not having done anything.

They will continue their fight to rescue the children in the brothels. There is still a lot to do. All I did was accompany them in this project that belongs to them. My project is to fight on my own ground, in Europe where the famous philosophy of "new love" has its roots.

In a few minutes I will pass the last customs control. The whole team is there, all twenty, waving their hands. Teelapon and Païthoon turn away.

Lao runs down the corridor, the customs official lets her pass. Her bony little hand gives me an envelope of blue cardboard paper, tears rolling down her face. I kiss the forehead of this sick child, perhaps for the very last time.

I hurry to reach the boarding gate, walking like a robot down the passageways of this gigantic airport. In the airplane I slump against the headrest. My memories overcome me, there are too many. The man sitting beside me, a charming man in his fifties on a business trip, is worried at my tears. I turn away from his gaze. I do not want to share my story. Not yet. It is too soon.

In my pocketbook my hand finds the thick paper of the letter the sick child gave me. I open the blue envelope. Inside there is just one sheet of paper with a childish drawing in crayon. I recognize the rescue home, the trees and the yard filled with the children's heads. And at the end of the garden, drawn in thick lines, a child sitting on the swing. Alone. The one that gave me this letter of farewell: "Lao."

Epilogue

WHAT WE CAN DO

The fight against child prostitution is not a lost battle. There are things we can do. Preventive measures can quickly be implemented:

- It is urgent that the ambiguity regarding pedophilia be brought out into the open and to fight to keep the concept of "new love" from becoming a triviality. Today it is easy to find books and magazines on the market that openly promote pedophilia. Is that so surprising seeing that networks and international clubs prosper and are respected? Remember: the law considers sexual aggression of a child a crime.

- Prevention: children, and parents, must be informed about the dangers incurred. Everyone involved in education, professors, teachers, sociocultural workers, etc., must play an important role in this information. It is quite common that pedophiles turn to educational institutions to be closer to children. Why not give thought to methods of detection that would make it possible to avoid hiring such teachers? In case of offense, these criminals should be prosecuted. It is deplorable that schools choose to cover personnel implicated for fear of scandal or permit them to continue teaching in another school, as is so often the case, without considering the trauma caused to the child and future risks. Medical personnel should also be adequately trained to recognize immediately cases of pedophilia.

- Little boys who are victims of rape should be given methodical follow-up until they reach adulthood. From the many declarations gathered, we were able to conclude that child abusers had often been abused themselves during the course of their childhood. The abused child becomes a child abuser. And the cycle of violence is continued.

- It is time to extend the care of sexual perverts more widely in Europe. The experience of the Pinel Center in Montreal is recognized by many professionals. Why not create departments specialized in the treatment of sexual delinquents both in prison and after their release? Why can't justice and medicine work together in this field, cooperating to treat sexual delinquents and thereby save other potential victims from being raped? One thing is clear: it doesn't do any good to throw a child abuser into prison without giving him psychiatric treatment, first of all because this kind of criminal is also often a man in distress, and secondly because once he has served his term, he is released and almost always will commit subsequent offenses.

- There is not enough collaboration between the various law enforcement agencies in this field. Too many habitual pedophiles travel unhindered to regions of the third world where they can give free reign to their mania without risking prosecution. Networks have been created to assure the promotion of criminal circuits. Guidebooks telling where to find children can be found on the racks of magazine stands even though the Convention for Children's Rights is meant for all children, rich and poor.

- Today, the pedophiles who once went to the Philippines or Sri Lanka are now found in Bangkok. They are often known to the local police or to their respective Ambassadors, but nothing is done to limit their abuse. European countries could exercise the necessary pressures on countries that are too tolerant regarding the exploitation of children for illegal work or sexual tourism. The International Labor Office in Geneva elaborated strategies aimed to help certain countries implement realistic and acceptable policies regarding child labor. Recommendations have already been made to the government of Thailand. Recently, the government of India accepted to review security measures concerning children working in rug factories.

You can help to support our actions in Bangkok. Three addresses:

- In France: Association Tomorrow, P.O.Box 136 301 Z, 34000 Montpellier. Mention CPCR, Bangkok

- In Belgium: Familles sans frontières, ASBL. Postal account No. 240 0860784-10. Tax deductible. Mention CPCR, Bangkok

- In Switzerland: White Lotus Foundation, Postal account No. 12-2048-5. Union des banques suisses, Geneva. Mention CPCR, Bangkok.

To reach us, write to: Marie-France Botte and Jean-Paul Mari, P.O.Box 3, 1180 Brussels 7, Belgium.

- Action against sexual tourism being carried out by the ACPE, 76 rue de la Verrerie, 75004 Paris should also be noted.

- For all information, contact the General Delegate for Children's Rights and Aid to Youth, WTC, Tower 1, 20th floor, 162 Boulevard Émile Jaquemin, 1210 Brussels. Tel. (33-2) 219 74 01 - Fax (32-2) 219 63 02.